I'm always on the lookout for ancient wisdom made ⟨...⟩ world. Not everyone does this well. Andrew Arndt d ⟨...⟩ gift in re-presenting "desert spirituality" for this gene ⟨...⟩ the nourishment your soul longs for.

> RICH VILLODAS, lead pastor of New Life Fellowship
> and author of *The Deeply Formed Life*

In *Streams in the Wasteland*, Andrew Arndt shares with us how the Desert Fathers and Mothers have shaped his own faith, welcoming us to listen as they still teach us about God, others, and our world. Set against a backdrop of Scripture, this book invites us all to experience the love and inner freedom described by Andrew's ancient friends.

> ALICE FRYLING, author of *Aging Faithfully: The Holy Invitation of Growing Older*

In Scripture, wilderness is where you find trouble. But it's also where we encounter the burning bush; it's the rugged country where God finds us and rescues us. In these pages, we hear—through a fresh and artful pen—these ancient voices who knew the wild places and the wild God. We're desperate for this wisdom.

> WINN COLLIER, director of the Eugene Peterson Center for Christian Imagination at
> Western Theological Seminary, author of *Love Big, Be Well* and *A Burning in My Bones*

Andrew Arndt has made friends with the Desert Fathers and Mothers, and he invites us to enjoy their friendship too. His winsome book reveals how their wisdom sheds light on the problems we face today. One to read, underline, ponder, and share.

> AMY BOUCHER PYE, author of *7 Ways to Pray*

Andrew is one of the clearest, brightest thinkers in the local church. This book takes us right into the presence of God, opening our eyes to the mystery and wonder of the resurrected Christ.

> BRADY BOYD, senior pastor of New Life Church

With one foot in the stream of the desert dwellers from the fourth and fifth centuries and the other in our contemporary spiritual wasteland, Andrew Arndt shares with his reader the treasures that desert spirituality offers us in our own seeking. As Andrew gently insists, exploring these treasures will not draw us into a privatized faith. Rather, they lead us into transformed relationships within our communities of faith and a more transforming engagement with God's world. This book will become a treasure for many seekers.

TREVOR HUDSON, author of *Seeking God: Finding Another Kind of Life with St. Ignatius and Dallas Willard*

In a cultural moment that chases celebrity and prizes originality, Andrew Arndt is calling us back to the hard-won wisdom of the wilderness. The monks and sages down through the ages have much to teach us if we will just listen. Simplicity. Sanity. Soul-satisfying anonymity. This book contains a great healing for our emaciated age.

DANIEL GROTHE, author of *The Power of Place*

In a time of fickle faith and rampant individualism, Andrew Ardnt will encourage your journey. But then his words will poke and prod you to the point of offense. This, I think, is the making of a great book, unafraid to tell the truth with grace, but to tell the truth no less. Solitude, community, and mission—this is the Jesus way, the way the desert disciples revealed to be our life-giving source for the journey. Andrew serves here as a wise guide into *that* way.

AJ SHERRILL, priest and author of *Being with God: The Absurdity, Necessity, and Neurology of Contemplative Prayer*

Andrew Arndt invites us, with his constant posture of honesty and grace, to be re-centered by the wisdom and practices of the Desert Fathers and Mothers. As they have led him, they will guide you toward the power and presence of community so you may kneel down once again at the riverbank of Living Waters.

ANDI ROZIER, pastor of worship at New Life East

Amidst global crises and faltering faith, many find themselves in the desert, disoriented and disappointed. Andrew Arndt shows us that we are not the first to feel this way. The desert saints stood against the corruption of the church and the pollution of the world, embracing and embodying a different wisdom. The brilliance of this book is not simply in the way Andrew selects and synthesizes from the desert saints; it's in how he places their insight into our lives like water on our parched tongues.

GLENN PACKIAM, lead pastor of New Life Downtown, author of *The Resilient Pastor* and *Blessed Broken Given*

STREAMS
in the
WASTELAND

Finding Spiritual Renewal
with the Desert Fathers & Mothers

ANDREW ARNDT

A NavPress resource published in alliance
with Tyndale House Publishers

NavPress ◗

NavPress is the publishing ministry of The Navigators, an international Christian organization and leader in personal spiritual development. NavPress is committed to helping people grow spiritually and enjoy lives of meaning and hope through personal and group resources that are biblically rooted, culturally relevant, and highly practical.

For more information, visit NavPress.com.

Streams in the Wasteland: Finding Spiritual Renewal with the Desert Fathers and Mothers

Copyright © 2022 by Andrew Arndt. All rights reserved.

A NavPress resource published in alliance with Tyndale House Publishers

NavPress and the NavPress logo are registered trademarks of NavPress, The Navigators, Colorado Springs, CO. *Tyndale* is a registered trademark of Tyndale House Ministries. Absence of ® in connection with marks of NavPress or other parties does not indicate an absence of registration of those marks.

The Team:
David Zimmerman, Publisher; Caitlyn Carlson, Editor; Elizabeth Schroll, Copy Editor; Olivia Eldredge, Operations Manager; Libby Dykstra, Designer

Cover illustration of God in Nature and Revelation, 1875, public domain.

Interior photograph of wood texture copyright © Chayanit/Rawpixel. All rights reserved.

Author photograph by Ashlee Weaver, copyright © 2018. All rights reserved.

Published in association with The Bindery Agency, www.TheBinderyAgency.com

Excerpts from *The Sayings of the Desert Fathers [Apophthegmata Patrum]: The Alphabetic Collection* by Benedicta Ward, SLG, trans., CS 59 (Kalamazoo, MI: Cistercian Publications, 1975) are used by permission of Liturgical Press. All right reserved.

Some of the anecdotal illustrations in this book are true to life and are included with the permission of the persons involved. All other illustrations are composites of real situations, and any resemblance to people living or dead is purely coincidental.

For information about special discounts for bulk purchases, please contact Tyndale House Publishers at csresponse@tyndale.com, or call 1-855-277-9400.

ISBN 978-1-64158-451-7

Printed in the United States of America

28	27	26	25	24	23	22
7	6	5	4	3	2	1

For the saints of Believers Church, Marshfield, circa 1981–1999,
who first showed me holiness. Your witness still inspires me.

Contents

Foreword

"WE ALWAYS, EVENTUALLY, BECOME LIKE WHAT WE WORSHIP."
These words house a warning, obviously, but they're also pregnant with promise. At one level, they call us back to the searing reality of God's holiness, pressing us to remember that God is not useful—never at our disposal, not in any sense a force we can wield or a power we can resource. At another level, however, they renew our confidence, reminding us that the God who always keeps his promises has promised to conform us to the image of his beloved Son (Romans 8:29).

This, then, is the warning: We become like what we worship; therefore, we must turn away from idols. And this is the promise hidden in the warning: We can, in fact, turn away from idols because God has turned his face to us. We have not only seen "the light of the knowledge of the glory of God in the face of Jesus Christ" (2 Corinthians 4:6, NRSV); we are also being "transformed into the same image from one degree of glory to another" (2 Corinthians 3:18, NRSV). In his light, we are becoming light.

———

God has made it possible for us to turn from idols, but that work can be done only in "the wilderness." Why? Because, as the Desert

Fathers and Mothers knew, it is only in no-man's-land that we come to the end of our competencies, our consolations, and our kinships. We cannot really love our neighbors—including, especially, our dearest friends and closest family—until we have been set free both from their control and our own fantasies and suspicions. We can live with them nonpossessively only as we are able to divest ourselves of unnecessary possessions. We can be present to them only if we know how to withdraw—for their sakes as well as our own—into the presence of the God who so often seems to be absent. As Andrew puts it in his preacherly (but not at all preachy) way:

> Abraham couldn't be a blessing to the world unless he
> first left his family. Moses couldn't deliver the people from
> their oppression unless he first threw off the trappings of
> Egyptian power. Rahab couldn't welcome the spies and
> save her family unless she renounced Jericho in her heart.

This, I believe, is the deepest wisdom of the desert: We have to turn not only from evil but also from the good as we have known it. We must learn what it means to say, "No one is good but God alone" (Mark 10:18, NRSV). We must discover why it is "more blessed to give than to receive" (Acts 20:35). We must know how to choose "the better part" (Luke 10:42, NRSV).

———

Maximus the Confessor, reflecting on Christ's stripping of the powers (Colossians 2:15), argues that Christ went out into the wilds in order to ensnare the devil: "He provoked, by means of our temptations, the wicked power, thwarting it by His own attack, and putting to death the very power that expected to thwart Him."[1] He stripped the powers of their power, Maximus says, by curing our nature, which he had assumed for us and our salvation, drawing out the "corrupting poison" of the devils' wickedness and "consuming it like fire."[2]

In the light of Maximus's reflections, we can see that Jesus was able to overcome evil because he never let an imagined good separate him from the reality of God. He could refuse to turn stones to bread because he had no illusions about his own competencies. He could refuse to throw himself down from the Temple because he did not doubt the Spirit's consolation. He could refuse control over the kingdoms of this world because he knew his kinship with the Father—and with us.

Thanks to his victory, we can live those refusals with him. But we must decide to live them! Andrew is right: We live in a spiritual wasteland because we have not yet joined Christ in his wilderness. So if we want to see the promised times of refreshment in our lives, then we need heed the wisdom of the desert, the wisdom of the Deserted One—turning aside to the cross that burns but does not consume, drinking deeply from the streams of living water that rush from the wounds of the Crucified One. All our hopes, all God's hopes, hang on us becoming like him.

Lent 2022
Chris E. W. Green
professor of public theology (Southeastern University)
and director of St. Anthony Institute for
Philosophy, Theology, and Liturgics

STANDING AT THE CROSSROADS

This is what the LORD says:
"Stand at the crossroads and look;
ask for the ancient paths,
ask where the good way is, and walk in it,
and you will find rest for your souls.
But you said, 'We will not walk in it.'"

JEREMIAH 6:16

A time is coming when men will go mad, and when they see someone who
is not mad, they will attack him saying, "You are mad, you are not like us."

ABBA ANTHONY

THE MAN APPROACHED ME after a worship service, and his story poured out. He'd been born and raised in a nonreligious home—had no spiritual background to speak of. He married young and started a business with his best friend. The company became very successful, very quickly. Then, after a decade or so, tragedy struck: His wife was diagnosed with breast cancer. They fought it with all their strength and all their resources—at times feeling like they had the upper hand in the battle; at others fearing that her precious life was slipping away.

Eventually, it did. The cancer metastasized and spread to her brain—pillaging her personality many months before it stole her life. She passed, leaving him behind with their two children. He returned to work only to discover that his friend had angled to push him out of the company they'd built together. Bereaved, betrayed, and grieving what had suddenly become of his life, with no spiritual foundation to speak of, he began to self-medicate to numb the pain. He entered a spiral of sadness and self-harm that would last several years.

"And so," he explained to me, "my girlfriend and I wandered in here a few weeks ago. I'm not even sure why, but we did. And every time I sit in these services, I find myself weeping in a way that I haven't since my wife passed. I just sit here and cry and cry. I don't know what's happening to me. And I don't even really understand what you guys are singing and talking about. But something is happening to me. And I know that it's good."

This man had stumbled across a well in the desert of his experience. He was finding God amid the desolation of his life. The existential hunger at the core of his life was being satisfied.

"Man is a hungry being," writes the Orthodox priest Father Alexander Schmemann. "But he is hungry for God. Behind all the hunger of our life is God. All desire is finally a desire for Him."[1] The psalmist said as much:

> You, God, are my God,
>   earnestly I seek you;
> I thirst for you,
>   my whole being longs for you,
> in a dry and parched land
>   where there is no water.
>
> PSALM 63:1

We are hungry, we are thirsty—for God. The desperate longing of our lives is for God. And we—as Saint Augustine said long ago—are "restless" until we find God.[2] Unsatiated spiritual restlessness is always to our hurt.

In time, as the man in my church found himself satisfied in God, he also found his sadness healed and self-harm at an end. His humanity was being and continues to be restored. As a pastor and friend to him, it's been a delight to watch. But my friend's story, I think, is also a parable for our time. Whether we know it or not, God is our inescapable environment, our first and final truth. But many—even in the church—are not really aware of this. The poet Rainer Maria Rilke referred to God as "a web / of tangled roots" plunged deep into the dark soil of our existence, out of whose "avid warmth," he said, "I rise."[3]

Such rising only really takes place when we recognize and embrace God amid the dark soil. In the absence of this, we will—each in our own way, to be sure—try to satisfy our hunger for God with what is not-God, with relationships and success, with sex and power, with prestige and pleasure of every kind.

I believe that the misidentification of spiritual desire combined with a staggering lack of practical knowledge about how such desire is satisfied is responsible for the madness of our time. It is responsible for things like codependency, promiscuity, and divorce; for the abuse of power, greed, and the senseless plundering of natural resources; for racism, classism, and sexism; for our pathological love of violence and fear of those who are different from us, as well as for every kind of substance abuse and destructive self-medication.

Less dramatically but no less insidiously, I believe that such misidentification is also responsible for the existential fatigue so characteristic of our age. Severed from our source, we are also cut off from any sense of purpose that might give meaning to our days. To use the language of the psalmist, we are like animals wandering about for food, howling because we are not satisfied (Psalm 59:15); and altogether too often, like animals, in our hunger we devour one another.

Ours is indeed a spiritual wasteland.

THE CROSSROADS

God's people are no strangers to this situation. We have been here before. Many times, in fact. In the sixth century BC, centuries of rebellion and wickedness finally began to catch up with the people of Judah and Jerusalem. The northern kingdom of Israel had already fallen to the Assyrians in the mid-late eighth century BC, but what should have served as a cautionary tale for the southern kingdom of Judah instead became a point of pride. The people of Judah simply reasoned that they were *better* than their northern counterparts. They believed they were safe.

To the complacent southern kingdom, God sent the prophet Jeremiah with the words, "From the north disaster will be poured out on all who live in the land" (Jeremiah 1:14). Judah's sense of safety was an illusion. Disaster was coming.

And what was the source of this disaster? The Lord asked Judah:

> What fault did your ancestors find in me,
>   that they strayed so far from me?
> They followed worthless idols
>   and became worthless themselves.

JEREMIAH 2:5

We always, eventually, become like what we worship—for better or for worse. We are, by an infallible law of the universe, transformed into the likeness of the objects of our devotion. The idols of the nations, under whose spell Judah had fallen, were "worthless." The Hebrew word for this is *hevel*—empty, futile, capable of nothing. Judah has exchanged their glorious God for facsimile gods; they've given up the living God for knock-off deities. And as the people of Judah gave themselves over to these idols, they "became worthless themselves."

The Lord puts the matter in the sharpest possible relief:

> My people have committed two sins:
> They have forsaken me,
>   the spring of living water,
> and have dug their own cisterns,
>   broken cisterns that cannot hold water.

JEREMIAH 2:13

There are moments in Scripture where moral and spiritual insight rise from the page like a volcanic island out of the heart of the sea. This is one of them. Jeremiah's words are a constant provocation to me. These two sins are the same for individuals, for families, for communities, peoples, and nations:

1. forsaking God, the only possible source of life; and
2. digging our own cisterns, which cannot hold water.

The consequences of living waywardly are not arbitrary. God is not a needy, insecure tyrant who lashes out with violence when he is ignored. No, we face the organic consequence of our choices. Should a thirsty man wonder that he dies when water is offered but he refuses to drink it? Should a starving woman wonder that she dies when food is offered but she refuses to eat it? Should we wonder that we die when Life is offered and we refuse to receive it?

But that is *exactly* what we do. And what's worse is, in our pride, we double down on our decisions. We feel the need to convince those around us—ourselves included—that the way we have chosen really is paradise:

> From the least to the greatest,
>   all are greedy for gain;
> prophets and priests alike,
>   all practice deceit.
> They dress the wound of my people
>   as though it were not serious.
> "Peace, peace," they say,
>   when there is no peace.
> JEREMIAH 6:13-14

We spend money we don't have on things we don't need and call it affluence. We work eighty hours a week at the expense of our families and call it #livingmybestlife. We pay our hourly employees the bare minimum and call it profit optimization. We starve ourselves and exhaust our bodies and call it health. We break faith with our spouses and children and call it "finding myself." Our personal lives and the life of our society together are one gigantic open wound, and we call it *peace.* In Hebrew, this word is *shalom,* the state of universal flourishing when everything in the created order is aligned as God intends, working as God intends. What Judah was doing, what *we* are doing, however much we try to call it "shalom," is anything but.

The prophet's job is to expose illusions, to rip the Band-Aid off so that we can feel the pain that compels us to seek the healing we need. Which is what Jeremiah does. If the diagnosis is "[We] have forsaken [God], the spring of living water, and have dug [our] own cisterns, broken cisterns that cannot hold water" (Jeremiah 2:13), the prescription is:

> Stand at the crossroads and look;
>   ask for the ancient paths,
> ask where the good way is, and walk in it,
>   and you will find rest for your souls.
>
> JEREMIAH 6:16

A RADICAL WAY

The paradox of the crossroads is that the only way to go forward is to go backward. To return to your roots, to the wisdom you once knew but had somehow forgotten. Jeremiah understood this. Judah was suffering spiritual amnesia. She had forgotten things that ought to have never been forgotten. As a result, her life had become not only "worthless" but monstrous. To go forward, she would have to go backward, to her covenantal roots, to a core of sanity that lay beneath the centuries of accumulated madness and folly.

Judah did not heed Jeremiah's warnings. Jerusalem fell to the Babylonians.

Centuries later, another society was teetering. Toward the end of the third century AD, the Roman Empire was a vast and powerful network of provinces, territories, and colonies, which had been united under the so-called *Pax Romana*—the Peace of Rome. The *Pax* had brought unprecedented security, prosperity, and unity to an enormous number of people. Her emperors were worshiped as gods. And why shouldn't they be? Through them, a kind of "salvation" had come.

But beneath the glamour of Rome, moral decay was setting in. Some of her sharpest minds knew it—and tried to call attention to it, to no avail. The Roman satirical poet Juvenal in the second century observed that the vitality of Rome's commonwealth was being sapped by what he called "bread, and the games of the circus"—the people's preference for entertainment above the cultivation of virtue and civic responsibility.[4] In Rome's decadent, entertainment-driven culture, human lives were routinely and unreflectively degraded in gory spectacle to amuse the chronically bored—the gladiatorial games being perhaps the most obvious and lurid example, where criminals, prisoners of war, and slaves would fight to the death for the entertainment of the masses. And all this so-called peace took place under the protection of the overwhelming military might of Rome, which maintained order by publicly crucifying dissidents.

Amid the decay, however, a group of people was bearing witness—often at the cost of their lives—to a better way. Since the mid-first century, from the same lands and the same people to which Jeremiah had once prophesied, a new way of being was sprouting up from the dark soil of the old. They claimed as their leader a man named Jesus—a Jewish prophet, teacher, and miracle worker, who had himself been crucified by Roman hands as a political threat and who, according to the reports of his followers, had been miraculously raised to life again by the power of Israel's God. His resurrection was seen as the decisive validation of the truth of his life and a declaration of his universal lordship.

From the very beginning, there was something refreshingly peculiar about these people. They were different. Believing that their founder was not dead but powerfully alive, intimately present, and still working wonders, they followed him. Their lives were rooted in the most ancient path possible: love—for God, for self, for neighbor, and for the created order—expressed in prayer and worship; in sexual purity and chastity; in shared living and generous hospitality; in self-denial and service; in affectionate devotion to one another and care for the poor; and in truthful speech and prophetic action, all directed toward the goal of seeing, in some small way, God's Kingdom on earth at it was (and is) in heaven.

So living, they stood out among their neighbors, friends, and business colleagues, and they began to gain followers. While the early Christians were often accused of being subversive or seditious (like their Master), upon scrutiny, their way of life regularly proved wholesome.

In short, the Christians were *good*—with a goodness that sprang from their devotion to Jesus and issued in lives that were notable for their integrity and generosity toward outsiders. Toward the end of the second century, the church father Tertullian remarked that followers of Jesus made manifest their difference in the care they showed not only their own vulnerable members but *any* "boys and girls who lack property and parents . . . for slaves grown old and ship-wrecked mariners . . . for any who may be in mines, islands or prisons," resulting in their pagan neighbors saying, "Look!"[5] The world, whether it knew it or not, saw the Lord Jesus in the faithful witness of the church.

A few short decades later, when plague began to ravage the Roman Empire, leaving masses of people dead or dying, Cyprian of Carthage could be heard exhorting God's people not to try to *explain* the plague but to instead *respond* to it in a manner worthy of their calling: namely by doing works of justice and mercy for those affected by the plague—and this during a time of intense persecution for the church![6]

It was this "way"—the radical way of Jesus—that slowly but surely won over the Roman Empire. From its meager beginnings of a hundred and twenty in the upper room (Acts 1:15), to perhaps ten thousand at the end of the first century, Christianity grew to five or six million people by the time of the emperor Constantine. The Jesus Way was a resounding success.

INTO THE WILDERNESS

But "success" often does funny things to a movement. Before long, if you're not careful, the radicality and potency that once made it attractive will begin to ebb. The movement becomes a *victim* of its own success. As Christianity grew in numbers, finding not only legal protection but honor and prestige under Constantine, many worried that it had begun to lose its soul. And so, as the first Christians had once revolted against the illusions of the *world*, a group of men and women now revolted against the illusions born of Christianity's *success*.[7] They retreated into the wilderness—to the deserts of Egypt, Syria, Palestine, and Arabia—to recover the radical way of Jesus that had initially marked the early church.

We know them as the Desert Fathers and Mothers. They retreated not in scorn or contempt but because, to them, the God revealed in Jesus was "so Holy, so great, possessed of such a love, that nothing less than one's whole being could respond to it."[8]

And respond with their whole being they did. Their lives became radiant, and through them the Spirit began to move upon the church in a fresh way. David Bentley Hart remarks that "it was from them that another current opened up within Christian culture: a renunciation of power even as power was at last granted to the church, an embrace of poverty as a rebellion against plenty, a defiant refusal to forget that the Kingdom of God is not of this world."[9] Before long, men and women from every corner of Christendom began to travel, sometimes from hundreds of miles away, to seek out the wisdom of the fathers and mothers and plant it like seed in their own lives, trusting the Lord to make the barren places fruitful again.

Much of their wisdom is recorded for us. They remind us, as Macarius the Great did, that our salvation and the posture of our hearts toward other people are bound up with one another: "Do no evil to anyone, and do not judge anyone. Observe this and you will be saved."[10] They help us recall, as Amma Sarah does, that learning to die daily to self is indeed the only way to ascend to holiness: "I put out my foot to ascend the ladder, and I place death before my eyes before going up it."[11] They teach us, as Abba Poemen did, that duplicitous speech is everywhere to be avoided: "Teach your mouth to say what is in your heart."[12] And that, as

Amma Theodora taught, God is seeking our good in all things, even the hard things: "So everything that goes against us can, if we wish, become profitable to us."[13]

And so it was that Christianity, which had once revolutionized the world, now began to re-revolutionize *itself* through the influence of the Desert Fathers and Mothers. By the example of their lives, they re-called the church to the radical way of Jesus. Their collected sayings eventually became the bedrock of the monastic movement, which spread throughout Europe and became a primary source of ongoing spiritual renewal as Europe descended into the Dark Ages. Their legacy of devotion to Jesus lit up the world—and it still does: a living testament to the truth that "the good life" is not to be found in this or that circumstance but in the ongoing experience of knowing the one whom Saint Francis of Assisi called "My God and my all."[14]

A PERSONAL WORD

I first became aware of the Desert Fathers and Mothers through the writings of folks like Richard Foster, Henri Nouwen, Thomas Merton, and others. Nouwen's *The Way of the Heart*[15] (which draws on the wisdom of the desert to teach us the disciplines of solitude, silence, and prayer) in particular had been a treasure of mine for many years. I learned a great deal from it, and as a young pastor, I returned to it and taught from it often. But it took a personal crisis to throw me into the depths of "desert" wisdom.

As I wrote about in my first book, *All Flame*,[16] our departure from the church we helped plant and pastor for seven years in Denver became for me an unexpected existential crisis. Leaving a city, a community, and work that I loved suddenly threw me into a personal space that I was not prepared for. Realizing how much my identity and sense of self-worth had been built on what I did in Denver, leaving it behind for a new city and a new call felt, in all honesty, like being put in a witness protection program. *Who even is "Andrew Arndt" apart from the reputation I built in Denver?* I wondered often. The transition from Denver to Colorado Springs in May 2017 stripped me bare.

It was providential, therefore, that Benedicta Ward's translation of *The Sayings of the Desert Fathers* wound up in my hands. Truthfully, I can't remember *how* it happened. Just *that* it did. And the hand of God was certainly on it.

As I cracked the book open and began to read, I found myself routinely astonished and comforted. In the midst of what felt like a great spiritual poverty (which I was having tremendous difficulty coming to grips with), here was a group of men and women who voluntarily *embraced* spiritual poverty, seeing it as the only sure path to God. What I had seen as threat, they saw as opportunity. What I had seen as suffocating darkness, they saw as a spacious place of God's light and goodness. What I had seen as emptiness, they saw as fullness.

I quickly began to make a home for myself inside their sayings and the stories that came from their lives. They gave me language not only to *see* but to *embrace* the season I was in. Their wisdom charted my uncharted waters; they were, in their unremitting oddity, cartographers of the holy for me. When it felt like no one was clamoring for my voice anymore, I found comfort in the call given to Abba Arsenius: "Flee, be silent, pray always, for these are the source of sinlessness."[17] When I was no longer *giving* direction in a community of faith but instead *receiving* it, I found help in the example of Abba John the Dwarf, whose superior planted a dead branch in the ground and told John to water it every day until it bore fruit—which John did, and sure enough, after *three years* the branch miraculously bore fruit: the slow fruit of long surrender and blind obedience.[18] And when I was tempted to make foolish value judgments on the turn my story had taken, I found solace in the gentle admonition of Abba Benjamin, who said, "Walk in the royal way, measuring the landmarks without meanness."[19]

The fathers and mothers, in short, helped me claim the wilderness as a place of renewal. And that is what it became. Before long, I found my spiritual life bearing fruit in new and unexpected ways. I fell in love with the "wilderness."

What is more, the nature of my circumstance taught me that the "wilderness"—and the renewal available in it—is not "out there" somewhere; it is right here, right now, all around. In the desolations we experience—the loss of a job, the loss of a relationship, the sudden loss of purpose; projects that fail, plans that don't succeed, dreams that unexpectedly shatter; pain in our bodies, pain in our minds, pain in our spirits—*God can be found*. With the eyes of faith, we can claim the riven landscapes of our lives as holy ground, learning to worship God on scarred and broken earth.

But it is bigger than our personal lives. I have come to agree, and agree deeply, with Thomas Merton, who said that now, in the modern world, "Everywhere is desert. Everywhere is solitude in which man must do penance and fight the adversary and purify his own heart in the grace of God."[20]

The desolations which the fathers and mothers once searched miles and miles to find have come to our doorstep. Everywhere, we are surrounded by a spiritual wasteland. The promises of a consumer society—indeed, many of the promises being made by a consumer *church*, captive to the illusions of a consumer society—are proving empty, and the lives of many people, even (where we have bought into the lie) our own, are existentially empty as a result.

But the wasteland need not conquer us. Indeed, if we have eyes to see it, the wasteland can become for us a place of deepening, abundance, spiritual vitality, and even cultural renewal. Jesus went into the wilderness and emerged full of the Spirit. So did the Desert Fathers and Mothers. So can we. They can show us how.

I've written this book, friend, to help introduce you to the beauty of the wilderness, to the wisdom of the Desert Fathers and Mothers. Their words and the example of their lives can put us in touch, once again, with the radical way of Jesus Christ—which is the only hope not only for our own lives but for the life of the church and of our society.

The book is arranged in three parts—a grid for making sense of the call to the wilderness: (1) our relationship with God; (2) our relationship with others (that is, the call to community); and (3) our relationship with the wider world. Each chapter will be framed around a different component of what I'll call "desert spirituality." I'll draw out sayings and stories that help us locate the meaning of that component, show how it is rooted in the way of Jesus, and talk about how practicing it can help us live more humanly in an increasingly inhumane world.

A fair warning: Should you decide to live this way, it will make you *odd*. Abba Anthony's prophetic words prove themselves more and more with the passing of time: "A time is coming when men will go mad, and when they see someone who is not mad, they will attack him saying, 'You are mad, you are not like us.'"[21] But following the way of Jesus has always put us a bit out of step with the world. We are indeed "a peculiar people" (1 Peter 2:9, KJV), for we have seen something different—the Kingdom—and we are choosing to live in it, whatever it costs us. The quality of our beautiful, Christ-centered humanness will always strike the unbelieving world as odd—even "mad," which only exposes the world's own madness. But we know that our life depends on it. As Kentucky farmer Wendell Berry, one of the most prolific authors and social critics of our day (and also something of a Desert Father, in my opinion) put it: "To be sane in a mad time / is bad for the brain, worse / for the heart. The world / is a holy vision, had we clarity / to see it."[22]

And see it we must. The prophet Isaiah wrote, "The wilderness and the wasteland shall be glad . . . the desert shall rejoice and blossom . . . waters shall burst forth in the wilderness, and streams in the desert" (Isaiah 35:1, 6, NKJV), which bring healing and renewal to the thirsty ground.

But *everything depends on seeing*. As Isaiah says, "Behold!" (Isaiah 35:4, NKJV). Renewal is available to us *as we discern God in the wasteland*. And the Desert Fathers and Mothers can show us the way.

PART ONE

INTO THE DESERT WITH GOD

Here we begin to explore the call to the wilderness:

the spiritual horizon that guides our quest;

the renunciation of the heart that makes it possible;

and the practices that work the life of the Kingdom into us.

CHAPTER 1

FOR THE LOVE OF GOD

God is love. Whoever lives in love lives in God, and God in them.
1 JOHN 4:16

Abba Amoun of Nitria came to Abba Anthony and said to him,
"Since my rule is stricter than yours, how is it that your name is better
known amongst men than mine is?" Abba Anthony answered,
"It is because I love God more than you."
AS TOLD IN *THE SAYINGS OF THE DESERT FATHERS*

I GREW UP IN A SMALL TOWN in central Wisconsin called Marshfield—so named because, well, that's what it is: a network of marshes and swamps and bogs (bonus points if you know the difference between those three—or maybe *you* are from Marshfield, too?) and open fields as far as the eye can see. My siblings and I lovingly refer to Marshfield as "Marsh Vegas" or "Marshopolis," if only to underscore that the place really is as unspectacular as the name implies.

And yet, I knew some pretty spectacular people there. One of them was a guy named Bill. When his wife died of an incurable brain tumor in the mid-1980s, leaving him widowed with two small children, Bill resolved in his heart to be a man of unusual holiness, dedicating himself to prayer, to his children, and to his church. He owned and operated a small construction company, and so was able to work just as much as he needed to in order to meet his family's needs—which he intentionally kept to a minimum. The resulting freedom allowed him to give himself over to a life of deep devotion and ministry to the church. There was a kind of studied austerity about Bill; his lean frame matched his lean life—which, paradoxically, made Bill large with the ministry of the Spirit.

And what a ministry it was. Besides the time spent in prayer and fasting at his home (which he built just up the dirt road from the church), Bill spent hours in prayer at the church. We ran a little Christian school out of our church, and I remember frequently bumping into Bill while I was trekking across the sanctuary for one reason or another. Hands folded behind his back, head down, Bill would make circles around the sanctuary for hours, praying in tongues, interceding for the church and its leadership, watching and waiting, listening to the Lord.

Bill lived his life in the presence of God, and it showed. Our church's leadership frequently sought Bill out for spiritual insight. His words had *gravitas*, weight. When Bill began a sentence with, "You know, while I was in prayer the other day . . ." you listened; a word was coming that would cut right to the quick. When Bill prayed *for* you, somehow you knew that those prayers were going to make a difference. When Bill prayed *over* you, you buckled your seat belt—anything could happen.

And yet, for all that, do you know what I remember most about Bill? The kindness in his eyes. How when he looked at you, it felt like he really *saw* you. How his countenance opened to receive you. How, when he laid his hands on you, for all the spiritual power so evident in his life, he laid them *gently*, without any attempt to conjure a feeling or manufacture an experience. His awareness and confidence in God gave him an easy demeanor. His was a life given to the love of God.

Bill, in his own understated way, was a radical. A Desert Father for the modern era. One of the things that convinces me the way of life practiced by the Desert Fathers and Mothers is possible for us today is that the more I read them, the more they sound like people I know. For all their "otherness," they are familiar to me. I have known many of them. I know many still. And their lives are saturated with divine love.

A MONK'S OBJECTIVE

Sometime during the late fourth century, a young man by the name of John Cassian made his way down into the Egyptian desert to learn the ways of holiness from the great monks. Cassian was an educated man and was determined to not only learn but also to try to shape the teaching of the Desert Fathers and Mothers for a wider audience. After years of sifting, sorting, and organizing the material, Cassian wrote two books, *Institutes* and *Conferences*—the former a kind of handbook on the monastic life and the latter a more systematic philosophical treatise on the thought of the Egyptian fathers. In the early fifth century, Cassian founded a monastery near Marseilles (France), which put into practice what he had learned while in Egypt. This monastery also became a kind of template for later monastic movements, including that of Benedict of Nursia, whose famous "Rule of Saint Benedict" still influences Benedictine, Cistercian, and Trappist monks to this day. Cassian's careful distillation of the spirituality of the desert lives on.

What strikes the reader about the *Conferences* is the philosophical orderliness of it. The book is presented as a series of conversations with some of the most prominent figures of the Egyptian desert, and each conversation builds on the next in a more or less logical order. The first conversation is crucial, as it sets the foundation for all that is to come.

Sitting down with Abba Moses, one of the most compelling Egyptian monks, John Cassian and his friend Germanus engage Moses on the life of the Spirit. "Every art," Moses begins, "and every discipline has a particular objective, that is to say, a target and an end peculiarly its own."[1] Moses then goes on to describe the hardships and toils that farmers, businesspeople, and professional soldiers endure—doing it all for the sake of their objective: an abundant harvest, the hope of profit, military glory. In the same way, Moses tells them, the monk endures for a single goal, a single objective. And just what is that objective?

The aim of our profession is the kingdom of God . . .
but our point of reference, our objective, is a clean heart,

without which it is impossible for anyone to reach our target.[2]

So, according to Moses, where we are *headed* is the Kingdom of God (our aim, or our goal), but our *objective* (or what we are trying to achieve via the habits and practices of the desert) is a clean heart, a pure heart. He continues:

> Everything we do, our every objective, must be
> undertaken for the sake of this purity of heart. This
> is why we take on loneliness, fasting, vigils, work,
> nakedness. For this we must practice the reading of the
> Scripture, together with all the other virtuous activities,
> and we do so to trap and to hold our hearts free of the
> harm of every dangerous passion and in order to rise step
> by step to the high point of love.[3]

Did you catch that? The pure heart for Moses is ever rising "step by step to the high point of love." The goal of desert spirituality is one thing: love. And if you miss that, you miss the whole thing.

> Fasting, vigils, scriptural meditation, nakedness, and
> total deprivation do not constitute perfection but
> are the means to perfection. They are not themselves
> the end point of a discipline, but an end is attained
> through them. To practice them will therefore be useless
> if someone instead of regarding these as means to an
> end is satisfied to regard them as the highest good. . . .
> The demands made on the body are actually only the

beginning of the road to progress. They do not induce that perfect love which has within it the promise of life now and in the future. And so we consider the practice of such works to be necessary only because without them it is not possible to reach the high peaks of love.[4]

FOR THE LOVE OF GOD

Oftentimes the impression we have (if we have one at all) of the Desert Fathers and Mothers is of a group of austere, somber, joyless folks living basically solitary lives, mostly because they couldn't stand to be with people—extreme introverts seeking religious justification for their contempt for society. Though this was certainly the case with some of them (many would have been absolutely terrible guests at a dinner party), the most clear-minded and spiritually vibrant among them show us by word and example that the goal of the spiritual life is one thing: love. In fact, they thought that lovelessness was a sure sign of either spiritual immaturity or that something had gone disastrously wrong in the spiritual life. If you don't love, you just don't *get it*—"it" being God and his Kingdom. At all.

And of course this is precisely what the New Testament teaches us. As the apostle Paul wrote,

> If I speak in the tongues of men or of angels, but do not have love, I am only a resounding gong or a clanging cymbal. If I have the gift of prophecy and can fathom all mysteries and all knowledge, and if I have a faith that can move mountains, but do not have love, I am nothing. If I give all I possess to the poor and give over my body to hardship that I may boast, but do not have love, I gain nothing. . . .

> These three remain: faith, hope and love. *But the greatest of these is love.*
> 1 CORINTHIANS 13:1-3, 13, EMPHASIS MINE

The greatest thing. Love.

As you read Paul's epistles, you see that every chance he got, he made love the centerpiece of the spiritual life of the church. To the Philippians, he wrote:

> And this is my prayer: that your love may abound more and more in knowledge and depth of insight, so that you may be able to discern what is best and may be pure and blameless for the day of Christ, filled with the fruit of righteousness that comes through Jesus Christ—to the glory and praise of God.
> PHILIPPIANS 1:9-11

To the Ephesians, he wrote:

> Follow God's example, therefore, as dearly loved children and walk in the way of love, just as Christ loved us and gave himself up for us as a fragrant offering and sacrifice to God.
> EPHESIANS 5:1-2

And to the Thessalonians, he wrote:

> Now about your love for one another we do not need to write to you, for you yourselves have been taught by God to love each other. And in fact, you do love all of God's

family throughout Macedonia. Yet we urge you, brothers
and sisters, to do so more and more.

1 THESSALONIANS 4:9-10

Love is the purpose. Love is the goal. Love is what it's all about.
One of Jesus' best friends, John, who knew the love of God
made manifest in Jesus as well as anyone, put like this:

> Dear friends, let us love one another, for love comes from
> God. Everyone who loves has been born of God and
> knows God. Whoever does not love does not know God,
> because God is love. . . .
>   Whoever lives in love lives in God, and God in them.
>
> 1 JOHN 4:7-8, 16

John's words leave us with absolutely no wiggle room—if
you don't love, you don't know God because God's very *essence* is
love. Period. Full stop. And, of course, all of this was simply an
ongoing *exploration of* and *elaboration on* the teaching of Jesus
himself, who said not only that the whole Old Testament could
be summed up by the commands to love God and one another
(Matthew 22:40) but also that by love and love alone the world
would know that we belong to him (John 13:35)—to him who
is Love Incarnate.

This is what the Desert Fathers and Mothers—at their best—
were after: the pure heart, the stripping away of *everything in their
lives* that did not serve the purpose of love, the destruction of
everything in their hearts that blocked or hindered the flow of the
love of God in their lives. Love was what drew them to the desert.
Love was the goal of their ongoing spiritual efforts. Everything

they did was undertaken for the love of God and others. The point of spiritual discipline for them was the disciplining of the heart for this one thing: *love*.

A fantastic example of this is that of Abba Amoun, who came to Abba Anthony one day and said, "Since my rule is stricter than yours how is it that your name is better known amongst men than mine is?" To which Abba Anthony answered, "It is because I love God more than you."[5] The story should make you chuckle. I laugh every time I read it. I mean, where does Anthony get off saying something like that? But of course he *can* say it—and say it without a trace of hubris—because it is quite simply the truth. Amoun was stricter with himself; Anthony is happy to concede the point. But Amoun had missed the goal and purpose of the spiritual life. That purpose was love. Anthony got it. And his life was radiant with love.

The story illustrates precisely what Abba Moses sought to convey to Cassian and Germanus: that strictness or severity of one's "rule" (the set of commitments a monk made that ordered their lives) was not the goal of the spiritual life. The "rules"—the patterns of fasting and prayer and self-denial and devotion—were put in place to help guide the heart into a greater love for God and neighbor. Without that overriding goal, they were sure to degenerate into self-justifying demonstrations of religiosity. But *with* that goal in place, the spiritual disciplines served as trellises by which the vine of the heart grew up, fanned out, and became fruitful in love.

And Anthony's own life demonstrates it well. Though he was certainly known for profound acts of self-denial, he was ultimately *better* known for a rare quality of tenderness, of care for others, of gentle love. As he served as a spiritual father to a handful of monks, Anthony's leadership was marked by wise and gentle care. Consider the following story:

> A hunter in the desert saw Abba Anthony enjoying himself with the brethren and he was shocked. Wanting to show him that it was necessary sometimes to meet the needs of the brethren, the old man [Anthony] said to him, "Put an arrow in your bow and shoot it." So he did. The old man then said, "Shoot another," and he did so. Then the old man said, "Shoot yet again," and the hunter replied, "If I bend my bow so much I will break it." Then the old man said to him, "It is the same with the work of God. If we stretch the brethren beyond measure they will soon break. Sometimes it is necessary to come down to meet their needs." When he heard these words the hunter was pierced by compunction [meaning that he was cut to the heart] and, greatly edified by the old man, he went away. As for the brethren, they went home strengthened.[6]

How we treat people matters. Our care for people is the measure of our devotion, a sure and inviolable index of our love for God. Jesus and the apostles taught that. So did Anthony: "Our life and our death is with our neighbor. If we gain our brother, we have gained God, but if we scandalize our brother, we have sinned against Christ."[7] Of Abba Anthony's teaching, one of the most prolific theologians of our day, the former Archbishop of Canterbury Rowan Williams remarks that "winning" our brother or our sister is not about "getting them signed up to something or getting them on your side." It is, rather, about "opening doors for them to healing and wholeness. Insofar as you open such doors for another, you gain God, *in the sense that you become a place where God happens for somebody else.*[8] "What is to be learned in the desert," he says, "is clearly not some individual technique for communing with the divine but the business of becoming a means of reconciliation and healing for the neighbor."[9]

And that very thing—becoming a means of healing and reconciliation for the neighbor—is just what the Desert Fathers and Mothers were known for. On one occasion, some old men in the community brought a young woman, pregnant out of wedlock, to Abba Ammonas, a disciple of Anthony's who had become a bishop in the community. They wanted him to give her a penance. Instead, he made the sign of the cross on the young woman's womb and ordered that six pairs of fine linen sheets be given to her. The old men were stunned. "Why did you do that?" they asked. "Give her a punishment," they demanded of him. Ammonas replied, "Look, brothers, she is near to death; what am I to do?" Ammonas knew that no punishment could be worse than the shame and fear that the woman felt. What was needed was not judgment but mercy. At his words, the old men departed, speechless, their accusations shattered by Ammonas's tenderness toward the young woman.[10]

A loving, tender heart toward others—that's what we're trying to cultivate. If we don't have that, nothing else matters. Abba Agathon remarked that "a man who is angry, even if he were to raise the dead, is not acceptable to God."[11] In the same spirit, Abba Moses counseled that we should

do no harm to anyone, do not think anything bad in
your heart towards anyone, do not scorn the man who
does evil, do not put confidence in him who does wrong

to his neighbour, do not rejoice with him who injures his neighbour. . . . Do not have hostile feelings towards anyone and do not let dislike dominate your heart; do not hate whom who hates his neighbour.[12]

Think about that. The kind of heart that we are trying to cultivate is not only one in which there is no dislike whatsoever—but even more, it is one in which there is *no dislike for the person who dislikes others*. This kind of love is capable of tender affection for everyone. Like God's love is—the kind of love that finally makes lovers out of the loveless.

A WORLD DEVOURING ITSELF

I think we need to pause here for a moment and reflect on how crucial this all is given the world that we live in—a world that is always all too capable of alarming acts of hatred.

On January 6, 2021, in Washington DC, a violent and angry mob stormed the United States Capitol building. Breaking through police barricades, dozens of people stampeded into our nation's seat of power (many of them, ironically, carrying crosses and placards saying, "Jesus saves"), attempting *at least* to protest and *at most* to overturn the results of the recent presidential election. Five people died in the melee.

The moment, for me at least, was apocalyptic, in the sense that it revealed (the Greek word *apokaluptó* means "to uncover" or "to reveal") a great deal that is wrong not with *them* (whoever was and is responsible for the riot) but with *us*. For of course the fracas of January 6 was only the latest in a line of recent outbursts in our country—outbursts that, it absolutely must be said, cut across party and ideological lines. As many sociologists are noting, we are more "tribal" than ever as a culture, building our universe of meaning on the notion that "we" (whoever "we" are) are good and that "they" (whoever "they" are) are bad, and that in truth, the world would be better off without "them." As Greg Lukianoff and Jonathan Haidt so brilliantly point out in their book *The Coddling of the American Mind*, the "cancel culture" that we live in is not in any way accidental but rather the predictable result of toxic tribalism and institutionalized contempt for the other that we have made a normal part of our lives.[13]

What is perhaps most alarming is that while the world is devouring itself with its suspicion, fear, and hatred, the church so often seems either unwilling or unable to stand against it. Indeed, in many quarters, the church is guilty of fanning the flames of hate, of providing fuel for the fire, of egging the culture on. When conservative Christians demonize Democrats and progressive Christians demonize Republicans—when it, in other words, takes a massive spiritual effort to acknowledge the image of God across the party line; even more, when it takes a massive spiritual effort to acknowledge that those who voted differently than we did might actually be brothers and sisters in Christ—we know we have huge problems on our hands. We've exchanged the worship of our glorious God for idols (Jeremiah 2:11). We've given our calling away.

And that calling is to be a people of love, a people who love with the love that heals and unites the world. What was ironic about those crosses at the riot on January 6 is that, according to the New Testament, the very thing that the cross of Jesus Christ saves us *from* is precisely our culture's endemic hatred and contempt for other people. Watch how Paul puts it in his letter to Titus:

At one time we too were foolish, disobedient, deceived
and enslaved by all kinds of passions and pleasures. We
lived in malice and envy, being hated and hating one
another. But when the kindness and love of God our
Savior appeared, he saved us, not because of righteous
things we had done, but because of his mercy. He saved
us through the washing of rebirth and renewal by the
Holy Spirit, whom he poured out on us generously
through Jesus Christ our Savior, so that, having been
justified by his grace, we might become heirs having the
hope of eternal life.

TITUS 3:3-7

Did you catch the progression Paul lays out there? The ultimate
manifestation of our "enslavement" to sinful passions and pleasures
is that we live "in malice and envy, being hated and hating one
another." By contrast, when the love of God made known in the
crucified and resurrected Jesus is poured into our hearts by the
power of the Holy Spirit, it goes right to the root of our wayward
passions and pleasures (such as the passion we have to be right, to
win; and the pleasure we take in seeing others suffer loss), destroy-
ing the antagonisms that enslave and divide us.

"Being hated and hating one another," friend, is simply what
unredeemed humanity *does*. It is Cain and Abel after the Fall of
Adam and Eve. It is the enmity of Jacob and Esau. It is the sad
and tragic history of Jew and Gentile, male and female, slave and
free. It is Israelis and Palestinians. Hutus and Tutsis. Democrats
and Republicans. The list could go on and on.

And this—*precisely* this—is what God in Christ saves us from.
Of the barrier between Jews and Gentiles (and he elsewhere extends

this to the barriers that exist between *everyone*) Paul writes, "For he himself is our peace, who has made the two groups one and has destroyed the barrier, the dividing wall of hostility. . . . His purpose was to create in himself one new humanity out of the two, thus making peace, and in one body to reconcile both of them to God through the cross, by which he put to death their hostility" (Ephesians 2:14-16).

This is what God in Christ has done and is doing by the power of the Spirit. And therefore the more we determine in our hearts to live in constant, deep proximity to God, the more we will be transformed into a people who ache for what God aches for—for healing, for restoration, for reconciliation, for peace. As Abba Nilus put it: "Prayer is the seed of gentleness and the absence of anger."[14] We become soft in our spirits toward other people. We begin to see them with the eyes of love. Our hearts begin to feel for them with the same tender love with which God in Christ has loved us and will always love us, from eternity to eternity. In our lives, the vicious circle of hate by which the world devours itself is broken, and redemptive love is released into the world, little by little—each act of love a living witness to the Kingdom that *is* and *is to come*, the Kingdom of divine Love that is Father, Son, and Holy Spirit, the Kingdom by which all things are made new.

ALWAYS LEADING US TO FRIENDSHIP

My friend Dave worked at an Episcopal church for a number of years. The church was large and had a fairly sizable pastoral and support staff comprised of people from all walks and seasons of life—people who loved each other and the church but also had differing perspectives on what was best for it. Staff meetings could be both energetic and, at times, highly contentious.

During one of the more contentious meetings, debate raged back and forth and lines were drawn in the sand until someone finally noticed that Father Art had been silent the entire time. Art was an Episcopal priest on staff in his latter years of life and ministry. A man who walked with God and had seen it all—conflicts, crises, schisms—and whose age and spiritual maturity meant he was never enamored with the *conflict du jour.*

"Father Art," they asked, "you haven't told us what you think. What's your opinion here? What do you think we should do?"

Art sat back thoughtfully in his chair for a moment and then finally leaned in toward the group and said, "I think that the Holy Spirit is always leading us into friendship."

The wise writer of Ecclesiastes said that "the quiet words of the wise are more to be heeded than the shouts of a ruler of fools" (9:17). Proverbs notes that "a gentle tongue can break a bone" (25:15). Art's wise, quiet, gentle words broke the tension in the room and made it possible for the contentious issue to be handled more constructively.

I think about that story often. It is an example to me of the kind of people we become when we walk with Jesus—namely, people whose disposition makes the Kingdom consistently manifest. And notice—and this is crucial to say—Art's words didn't paper over the differences present that day. Rather, *they made it possible for the differences to be handled in a way that built up and didn't tear down.*

I am afraid that many people in our day associate the call to love with a kind of sappy, whitewashing sentimentality that closes its eyes to the pain of the world and plugs its ears to the cries of the world while it wistfully hopes that someday, somehow, a global kumbaya-fest will spontaneously emerge. But this is not so. If what

Christians mean by "love" is whatever we see in the life, death, and resurrection of Jesus, then we know that the very *last* thing that love does is turn a blind eye to the world. This love is not conflict-avoidant. Indeed, it *leans into conflict*—like Jesus did. But it does so in a different way than the world does—courageously telling the truth while also being willing to suffer loss for the reconciliation of others; unmasking the powers that be while also pleading, as Jesus did, for those seeking our harm: "Father, forgive them, for they know not what they do" (Luke 23:34, ESV).

Perhaps no one in our time has expressed this fundamental thing as clearly, persuasively, and powerfully as Dr. Martin Luther King Jr., who, in the thick of the struggle for civil rights for Black Americans, said,

> To our most bitter opponents we say: "We shall match your capacity to inflict suffering by our capacity to endure suffering. We shall meet your physical force with soul force. Do to us what you will, and we shall continue to love you. We cannot in all good conscience obey your unjust laws, because noncooperation with evil is as much a moral obligation as is cooperation with good. Throw us in jail, and we shall still love you. Bomb our homes and threaten our children, and we shall still love you. Send your hooded perpetrators of violence into our community at the midnight hour and beat us and leave us half dead, and we shall still love you. But be ye assured that we will wear you down by our capacity to suffer. One day we shall win freedom, but not only for ourselves. We shall so appeal to your heart and conscience that we shall win *you* in the process, and our victory will be a double victory."[15]

That's it, right there. King understood what Abba Anthony knew so well: that "if we gain our brother, we have gained God." And of course, both were drawing on the teaching of Jesus, who said that if and when offense falls between us and a brother or sister, we ought to seek to resolve it *immediately* (Matthew 5:23-26)—and that we ought to not only love our brothers and sisters but even (and especially!) our enemies, with the same perfect and perfecting love that God the Father has and forever is showing us in Jesus the Lord (Matthew 5:43-48). This love made us who were once enemies the very friends of God (Colossians 1:21-22).

So it comes down to this: The spiritual life is about love. If we don't understand that, or if we lose sight of it, we'll miss the whole thing. But make no mistake—growing into a person of love does not happen accidentally. It takes hard work—a lifetime of it, in fact. Which is why Abba Moses concludes his discussion with Cassian and Germanus by insisting that while spiritual discipline is not the *point* of the spiritual life, it is nevertheless *indispensable*:

> Every hour and every moment working over the earth of our heart with the plough of Scripture, *that is, with the memory of the Lord's cross*, we shall manage to destroy the lairs of the wild beasts within us and the hiding places of the venomous serpents.[16]

The Cross makes this way of life possible. And—as the fathers and mothers of the desert knew so well—not just Jesus' cross but also the many crosses *we* are called to carry on the way to the Kingdom; crosses that free us *from* the world and *for* the Kingdom.

CHAPTER 2

THE GREAT RENUNCIATION

*May I never boast except in the cross of our
Lord Jesus Christ, through which the world has
been crucified to me, and I to the world.*

GALATIANS 6:14

*Have the mentality of an exile in the place where
you live . . . and you will have peace.*

ABBA POEMEN

WHEN I FIRST GOT TO KNOW OLA, a tiny little German woman in my hometown, she was in her early eighties and was—in our community at least—a living legend. Stories of the profound and miraculous went hand in hand with the mention of her name. Like the time Ola was visiting the Christian school that belonged to our church, and as she chatted with one of the fifth-grade girls, the girl spontaneously began speaking in tongues—which the girl had never done before—*even though Ola hadn't been talking about speaking in tongues*. Or the many times she prayed for folks who were sick or had chronic illnesses and saw them instantaneously healed. Or the time she was attending a prayer meeting and had a vision of Jesus. When she stood up to ask the others present if they could see him, they fell down under the power of God. In exasperation, she turned to the other side of the room to ask if *they* could see Jesus. Likewise, they hit the deck. Finally, she asked the man leading the prayer meeting if *he* could see Jesus. Ditto. Ola was left standing there, alone, with her gaze fixed on Jesus—in many ways, an apt image for her life.

Stories like this followed Ola wherever she went. She was a woman radiant with God. You could feel it when you were around her. I vividly remember the first time she came and spoke to my class at the Christian school. When she was done sharing from the Scriptures in the most simple and straightforward way, she asked if she could pray for us. Knowing Ola's reputation, we gladly said yes. One by one, tiny Ola—shorter than me and most of my fourth-grade classmates—went around and prayed for each of us. The weightiness of the divine presence on her was palpable. As she gently laid hands on each of us, each of us—like those at the prayer meeting—hit the deck. I remember being "out" (that was the way we talked about it in our charismatic church) for more than an hour, the presence of the Spirit washing over me in waves. It was an experience I'll never forget.

When I was eighteen and several weeks away from getting married, my mom encouraged Mandi and me to visit Ola in her little apartment. Her physical strength had very much waned in her later years, but her spirit remained strong to the end. She glided easily back and forth in her rocker that afternoon—heavily marked Bible sitting open on the TV tray in front of her—asking us about our relationship and what we were hoping for out of the future and sharing with us easily and naturally about God and her relationship with God. None of the miraculous fireworks accompanied our visit with Ola that day, but we knew that we were in the presence of a genuine saint and that those moments with her would remain with us forever. She sent us out with a blessing.

Defying everyone's expectations, Ola lived another nine years after our visit, just seven months short of one hundred years old. Her passing, quite honestly, felt like the passing of Moses on Mount Nebo (Deuteronomy 34)—her crossing over into the fullness of the divine presence represented (and still represents) a kind of passing of the torch to those of us who had been touched by her life.

I have shared often about Ola from the pulpit over the years— something about the disparity between her physical and spiritual stature strikes me as a marvelous bit of a divine humor, and it really does make for a good story during a sermon. During my preparation for one sermon, it suddenly occurred to me that I knew nothing of Ola's conversion experience. How, I wondered, did Providence conspire to create such a woman? I called my mom, who had known her well, to find out.

As the story goes, Ola had been a believer for most of her life.

She had faith—yes. But not a very vibrant faith. When she was in her sixties, her husband died. The experience suddenly placed her at a crossroads. Should she seek remarriage? Or walk a different path? When she made it a matter of prayer, the voice of the Spirit began to whisper to her to not seek a husband. Well, what then? The answer: "Marry Jesus."

And, in a way she had never done before in her life, Ola let go of all other loves for the love of Jesus. She put the ring on her finger, crossing the threshold into a life of complete dedication to the Lord, and never looked back. Renouncing all other loves, she cleaved solely to Jesus for the rest of her life. The result was a generous heart full of the love of God and a life radiant with the freedom and power of God.

THE CURIOUS FREEDOM OF THE DESERT

Love, *generosity*, *power*, and *freedom* are all excellent words we could use to describe the life and witness of the Desert Fathers and Mothers—especially *freedom*. Indeed, their inner freedom is so profound that it is at times shocking. But it is foundational to their way of life. We won't understand them—or the life that we also have been called to—until we come to grips with that freedom and where it comes from.

Here's a humorous story that I think illustrates their freedom well:

> It was said of Abba Agathon that he spent a long time building a cell with his disciples. At last when it was finished, they came to live there. Seeing something during the first week which seemed to him harmful, he said to his disciples, "Get up, let us leave this place."

But they were dismayed and replied, "If you had already decided to move, why have we taken so much trouble building the cell? People will be scandalized at us, and will say, 'Look at them, moving again; what unstable people!'" He saw they were held back by timidity and so he said to them, "If some are scandalized, others, on the contrary, will be much edified and will say, 'How blessed are they who go away for God's sake, having no other care.' However, let him who wants to come, come; as for me, I am going." Then they prostrated themselves to the ground and besought him to allow them to go with him.[1]

Agathon was one of the luminaries of the desert—an Ola figure to be sure—colorful, magnetic, and often surprising. This story captures his essence. Put yourself in the scenario: You've spent a year or so building your dream house, only to abandon it upon the first sight of something displeasing or harmful. You'd either have to be mad (which is what Agathon's disciples worried people would say: "Look at them . . . what unstable people!"), or *you'd have to be just that free*. Agathon insists that it is not instability but depth of perception and spiritual freedom that are driving his decision. Because he is not a slave to anything—not to his possessions, not to a place, not to his reputation, not to what anyone would think of him—Agathon is free to respond at the drop of the hat to the voice of the Spirit in his inner being. He is so free even from the need to have disciples that he places no pressure on them to follow him—he simply makes up his mind to obey God, and then he obeys. If they come, they come. If they don't, they don't. And he blesses them either way. (More leaders need to learn from his example.)

What is more, Agathon is *so free that the entire experience doesn't even seem dramatic to him.* He doesn't labor or agonize over the decision, as many of us would (I know I would). Faced with a sense that I was supposed to give my house away in an act of sacrificial obedience, I would surely travail over it in fasting and prayer, seeking counsel with friends and spiritual advisors for days and weeks and maybe months, just to be sure: *Are you really calling me to this, Lord?* (There is a place for this, by the way—we'll cover it later.)

Not Agathon. He simply sees the good to be done, the obedience to be offered, no matter the cost, and he does it. Just like that.

I say that the freedom of the Desert Fathers and Mothers is "curious" precisely because of how deep and pervasive it is. It goes all the way down to their depths and runs straight across the recorded tradition of their lives and sayings. It defines their whole manner of life. Of Abba Bessarion it was said that

> his life had been like that of a bird of the air, or a fish, or
> an animal living on earth, passing all the time of his life
> without trouble or disquiet. The care of a dwelling did
> not trouble him, and the desire for a particular place never
> seemed to dominate his soul, no more than the abundance
> of delights, or the possession of houses or the reading of
> books. But he seemed entirely free from all the passions of
> the body, sustaining himself on the hope of good things to
> come, firm in the strength of his faith.[2]

What a way to live. Entirely free from all the passions of the body, sustained on the hope of good things to come, firm in the strength of faith. Can you imagine what it would be like to live with that kind of inner liberty?

Freedom of spirit was a central pursuit of the Desert Fathers and Mothers. When someone tried to lure Abba Sisoes out of his dwelling place, Sisoes asked, "What are you saying to me . . . ? Was not the mere liberty of my soul enough for me in the desert?"[3]

For Sisoes, as for all those who fled to the desert, such freedom was the pearl of great price. It was what they fought and labored for. They were free from possessions, as we have seen. Free from the need to judge others. Free from the need to speak their minds. Free from the desire for power. Free from the desire to be honored by others. Free from their own reputations.

What is more, they were even free from their *outward forms* of freedom. Their flexibility in adapting themselves to the will of God, however it presented itself, is astonishing. So while they sought solitude, they received visitors in submission to the will of God as though they were receiving Christ. And while they were diligent in ordering their lives around rhythms of prayer and fasting, when those rhythms were interrupted by the demands of community life, they willingly entered those demands. And while they never, *ever*, actively sought positions of leadership, whenever it became clear that they were being genuinely called upon to lead others (through many objections, normally), they forsook their solitude and entered the call of God in obedience to Christ. *That free.*

The question is: How? What made that possible? What makes it possible for us?

ON RENUNCIATION

What made the freedom of the Desert Fathers and Mothers possible for them—and what makes it also possible for us—is something that I've come to call "the Great Renunciation."

Not long after their conversation with Abba Moses, John Cassian and Germanus (whom we met in the last chapter) sit down to talk with another of the "greats" of the desert—Abba Paphnutius—whose teaching will help them (and us) understand just what is involved in the quest to make the love of God the centerpiece of one's life.

Paphnutius begins his teaching first by outlining what typically draws people into the monastic life. He calls them three "vocations"—a word that can trip us up, since in modern usage we tend to (mis)identify the word *vocation* with *occupation*; that is, what we do for work. That's not what Paphnutius is talking about. The word *vocation* comes from the Latin *vocare*, which just means "to call." Paphnutius is about to tell us how God calls us to a deeper form of life.

In the first place, God does it directly, in the secret places of our hearts. "The vocation from God," Paphnutius says, "comes whenever some inspiration is sent into our sleepy hearts, stirring us with a longing for eternal life and salvation, urging us to follow God and to cling with most saving compunction to His commands."[4] And most of us know what this feels like. We sense God calling us to greater love and deeper obedience, and so, moved by the call, we begin to follow. Responding to the inner voice of the Spirit, we increase our time spent in prayer. We fast more. We bump up the percentage of our tithes and offerings in keeping with our growing income. We decide to open our home one night a week for a dinner where we can get to know our neighbors better. We become more intentional about cultivating spiritual friendships. This, according to Paphnutius, is the first form of God's call. But there is another form.

God also calls us through the witness of others. In Paphnutius's words: "The second type of calling is, as I have said, that which comes through human agency when the example and the advice of holy people stirs us to long for salvation."[5] This form tends to dovetail with the first form. And, once again, most of us also know what this feels like. Spiritual conversation with friends, leaders, pastors, mentors, or even reading spiritual books (ahem), open up for us new vistas of potential obedience, and so, moved by the call of the Spirit that now has come to us through the voice and witness of others, we begin to follow.

But there is yet another form of God's call—and I think this one holds the key to a great deal of transformation for us.

If we fail to be moved directly via the inner voice of the Spirit or through the life and witness of others, then God will seek to move us *indirectly* via what Paphnutius calls "necessity":

The third kind of vocation is that which comes through necessity. Imprisoned by the riches and pleasures of this world, we are suddenly put to the test. The danger of death hangs over us. The loss or seizure of our property strikes us. The death of those we love reduces us to sadness. And we are moved to turn in haste to the God whom we had neglected in the good times.[6]

What Paphnutius here is describing is the way that "necessity" or *circumstance* pushes us to new thresholds of surrender. And he is clear: While God would *prefer* that we are moved toward the Kingdom simply via the inner call of the Spirit or through the life and witness of others, he will *gladly* take what we give him out of the pain of necessity, using it to finally make us holy:

So it is the conclusion that counts. Someone committed by the beginnings of a glorious conversion can prove to be a lesser man because of carelessness, and someone constrained by some necessity to become a monk can, out of fear of God and out of diligence, reach up to perfection.[7]

Think of Ola—ambling along happily until the death of her husband forced a crossroads upon her. It seems to me that Paphnutius is putting his finger on an experience common to all of us—namely, feeling like we have been "checkmated" by the Lord via our circumstances.[8] Our once-solid health suddenly becomes shaky. The stock market takes a tumble and reduces our retirement savings to almost nothing. A beloved child becomes wayward, and we tragically lose touch with them. A business that we've labored to build over the course of a decade with a good friend goes sideways when that relationship crumbles. The death of a dream or of a loved one reduces us to ash. Suddenly we find ourselves reevaluating the meaning of life and asking entirely new questions. What is God saying to us in those moments? What is he calling us to?

Paphnutius suggests that God is calling us to something called "renunciation"—that is, a formal rejection of an old way of life in favor of a new way of life and being. He describes that renunciation as happening on three different levels:

The first renunciation has to do with the body. We come to despise all the riches and all goods of the world. With the second renunciation we repel our past, our vices, the passions governing spirit and flesh. And in the third renunciation we draw our spirit away from the here and the visible and we do so in order solely to contemplate the things of the future. Our passion is for the unseen.[9]

Paphnutius's three renunciations—and he is, in this way, emblematic of the entire tradition of the Desert Fathers and Mothers—are quite simply the call of discipleship. That call is entailed in the "Great Renunciation": our baptism.

THE GREAT RENUNCIATION

Not long ago, in the congregation where I serve as pastor, we baptized a young man in his twenties named Kevin. Kevin had spent most of his adult life in a place that was spiritually empty and increasingly desperate—lots of questions; no answers—and came to our church after a friend invited him. He loved it. In the weeks and months that followed, a newfound confidence in the person of Christ began to grow in him. He decided to volunteer with us. As he did, his confidence in Christ continued to grow, along with his love for our community, for the church (as did ours for him!).

Some of our leaders began to disciple him. Soon he expressed a desire to be baptized. We thought that sounded like a great idea. So on a Sunday morning, in front of the communion of saints in a high school gymnasium on the east side of Colorado Springs, we brought Kevin to the front. I said to the church: *Brothers and sisters, faith is the gift of God to his people. In baptism the Lord is adding to our number those whom he is calling. People of God, will you welcome Kevin and uphold him in his new life in Christ?*

The congregation responded: *We will.*

Then I turned to Kevin and said: *In baptism, God calls us out of darkness into his marvelous light. To follow Christ means dying to sin and rising to new life with him. Therefore I ask: Do you reject the devil and all rebellion against God?*

Kevin responded: *I reject them.*

I asked: *Do you renounce the deceit and corruption of evil?*

Kevin responded: *I renounce them.*

I asked: *Do you repent of the sins that separate us from God and neighbor?*

Kevin responded: *I repent of them.*

I asked: *Do you turn to Christ as Savior?*

Kevin responded: *I turn to Christ.*

I asked: *Do you submit to Christ as Lord?*

Kevin responded: *I submit to Christ.*

I asked: *Do you come to Christ—the Way, the Truth, and the Life?*

Kevin responded: *I come to Christ.*

I then made the sign of the cross with oil on his forehead and plunged him into the horse trough right there on the hardwood floor, baptizing him in the name of the Father, the Son, and the Holy Spirit. The congregation erupted with praise. A new life in Christ had begun.

GOD ALONE

This is what new life in Christ is predicated upon: rejection, renunciation, repentance. If we are baptized, we have stepped into a process that we will spend the rest of our lives coming to grips with. The inner voice of the Spirit, the witness of others, and the push and pull of circumstance will lead us ever deeper into purity of heart—that is, into love for God and others. Into the Kingdom.

Most of us, I am afraid, do not quite realize this when we first yield our lives to God. What we think is that we've done a kind of "one-off" thing that assures our standing with God. And yes, that is certainly true—there is a one-off quality to the life of faith. But it is also true that there is an "ongoingness" to our faith that will demand our whole lives. Watch how Paul puts it:

> Since, then, you have been raised with Christ, set your hearts on things above, where Christ is, seated at the right hand of God. Set your minds on things above, not on earthly things. For you died, and your life is now hidden with Christ in God. When Christ, who is your life, appears, then you also will appear with him in glory.
> COLOSSIANS 3:1-4

So far, so good. We *have been* raised. We *have died*. Our lives *are now hidden* with Christ in God. Signed. Sealed. Delivered. And yet, Paul goes on to say,

> Put to death, therefore, whatever belongs to your earthly nature: sexual immorality, impurity, lust, evil desires and greed, which is idolatry.
> COLOSSIANS 3:5

We *have died*, and yet we must continually *put to death*. We *have been raised*, and yet, as a matter of spiritual discipline, we must continually *set our minds and hearts* on those things that pertain to the reign of God in Christ. We *have* "put on" the new self (Colossians 3:10) but we must also *continually* "clothe [our] selves" (Colossians 3:12). And on and on it goes.

This side of the new heavens and the new earth, what God is doing is *continually* drawing our lives out of the old way of being and into the new way of being offered to us in Jesus—out of our entanglements, as Paphnutius says, with . . .

- the riches and goods of this world;
- our past, vices, and the pleasures of the flesh; and
- our obsession with "the here and the visible"

. . . so that we can be "all in" for God and his Kingdom.

Centuries later, the English anchoress Julian of Norwich reflected a similar idea. She claimed that our fleshly attachments result in a "doubtful fear" that God wishes to free us from—so that "we have most confidence in his delight and his love," becoming by this process of renunciation as increasingly "peaceful and restful" toward ourselves and others "as he is towards us."[10] In other words, as we let go, we become serene and strong in our love—which is the goal of the Christian life. The life of faith is a continual crossing of the threshold, a deepening of the Great Renunciation that is our baptism, a letting go of the things of this world so that we can attain the Kingdom. Until we arrive on the shores of the new creation, the process will never end.

One of the most poignant examples of this is that of the twentieth-century Trappist monk Thomas Merton. Merton's early years were marked by tragedy and a constant sense of spiritual homelessness. But in the late 1930s, Merton found himself drawn into the life of Christ. This is how he describes his conversion:

For now I had entered into the everlasting movement of that gravitation which is the very life and spirit of God:

God's own gravitation towards the depths of His own infinite nature, His goodness without end. And God, that center Who is everywhere, and whose circumference is nowhere, finding me, through incorporation with Christ, incorporated into this immense and tremendous gravitational movement which is love, which is the Holy Spirit, loved me.

And He called out to me from His own immense depths.[11]

Now it would be tempting to imagine that, with the repudiation of his old self and entry into the church, the quest was over for Merton. Not so: "For, although I was baptized . . . my human nature, my weakness, and the cast of my evil habits still remained to be fought and overcome."[12] His conversion was the first step into the land of freedom; the rest of his life would be an ever-deeper sojourn into it. As Paphnutius says, "So, then, the appearance of renunciation will be useless for us. It will be merely the body coming out of Egypt. More exalted and more valuable will be the renunciation by the heart."[13]

The years to come would teach Merton this. His conversion was followed almost immediately by a desire to submit himself completely to Christ and his Kingdom for the good of the world, which led to his taking vows to become a Trappist monk at the Abbey of Our Lady of Gethsemani in rural Kentucky. Merton describes an experience he had during one of his initial, exploratory visits to Gethsemani:

We crossed the court, climbed some steps, entered a high, dark hall. I hesitated on the brink of a polished, slippery floor, while the Brother groped for the light switch. Then, above another heavy door, I saw the words: "God alone."[14]

The symbolic value of this moment can hardly be overstated. Merton approaches the threshold of entry into his true vocation with an awareness that the deeper he presses into it, the truer the words "God alone" must and will prove to be. Like his baptism, his experience at Gethsemani would become a kind of daily pilgrimage that ushered him into the life and freedom of God and made his own life a blessing to the world. His book *The Seven Storey Mountain* concludes thus with these words: *Sit finis libri, non finis quaerendi*[15]—"The end of the book; not the end of the quest." The rest of Merton's life would be devoted to learning just what "God alone" truly meant. "True mystical experience of God," he wrote later in life, "and supreme renunciation of everything outside of God coincide."[16]

"Supreme renunciation," friend. That's the threshold we are daily called to—a renouncing of honor and power and prestige on the world's terms, a renouncing of what spiritual writer Fr. Ronald Rolheiser calls the "pleasure principle" as the guiding factor of our lives,[17] and a renouncing indeed of this entire visible world as the final good of our lives. We become like the heroes of faith in Hebrews 11:

All these people were still living by faith when they died. They did not receive the things promised; they only saw them and welcomed them from a distance, admitting that they were foreigners and strangers on earth. People who say such things show that they are looking for a country of their own. If they had been thinking of the country they had left, they would have had opportunity to return. Instead, they were longing for a better country—a heavenly one. Therefore God is not ashamed to be called their God, for he has prepared a city for them.

HEBREWS 11:13-16

THE PARADOX

But there's a paradox we need to understand about the heroes of faith in Hebrews 11: By *renouncing* the world—admitting that they were foreigners and strangers, by declaring that this world was not their own and letting go of their past—they *changed* the world. Abraham couldn't be a blessing to the world unless he first left his family. Moses couldn't deliver the people from their oppression unless he first threw off the trappings of Egyptian power. Rahab couldn't welcome the spies and save her family unless she renounced Jericho in her heart. These people were a transformative presence in the world *precisely because they lived in such a way that they were not captive to or defined by it.*

This is precisely what the Desert Fathers and Mothers are trying to teach us. "A brother asked Abba Poemen, 'How should I behave in the place where I live?' The old man said, 'Have the mentality of an exile in the place where you live . . . and you will have peace.'"[18] As Amma Sarah powerfully put it, "I put out my foot to ascend the ladder, and I place death before my eyes before going up it."

We might do even better to quote the apostle Paul: "May I never boast except in the cross of our Lord Jesus Christ, through which the world has been crucified to me, and I to the world"—the very crucifixion by which we are raised up into the new creation (Galatians 6:14-15). Only a people who have and are continually identifying themselves with the cross of Christ can really live for the love of God and others. Only the dead are free—and if we are baptized, then we *are* dead—to power, to reputation, to status, to *things*. The challenge is to claim it, daily, and to live into it.

The matter is of immense practical importance for our spirituality. I'll give you an example. An elderly woman in our congregation regularly gives large financial gifts to the church—in the tens of thousands of dollars. Each time she does so, she makes it clear that she wants the money used for the care of the widows, the orphans, the fatherless—the vulnerable of any and every kind in our congregation.

Surely, you think, this woman must be a wealthy heiress of some kind, casually writing checks to the causes and charities of her choosing while living on a vast estate, right?

Not so. The address in the upper left-hand corner of the checks isn't for some mansion but for an *apartment complex*. She's renounced all the usual trappings that come from wealth so that she can love those less fortunate than herself. Because this woman is not a slave to her money, because she has renounced it, died to it, she can be generous with it. And that is exactly what the desert tradition of renunciation is pointing us toward. When we're not slaves to things, we can be free for God and others. Love becomes the guiding principle of our lives.

I suspect that many of the great debates and antagonisms raging in the church today happen because we've failed to really embrace our identity as those who have and are daily called to the Great Renunciation. When I see how many Christians engage in questions of society, politics, race, gender, or theology, I find myself thinking, *Is this fear masquerading as righteous indignation?* Altogether too often our strenuous positions are but a thin veneer to cover our anxiety that the world is changing and that those things that once gave us a sense of security are being threatened. We're clinging tightly to something that gives us a sense of security and we will not, *cannot*, let it go—for fear that if we do, all will be lost.

The Desert Fathers and Mothers would tell us that, in anxiously trying to preserve our place, we prove we haven't renounced the world. Jesus would say that in trying to save our lives, we are bound to lose them (Matthew 16:25).

But the deeper we die to the world, the more freedom, courage, power, and love we will experience to engage those issues, and more, in ways that are genuinely helpful. When we lose our lives, we'll find them.

CHAPTER 3

ESSENTIAL HABITS FOR THE WITH-GOD LIFE

*Very early in the morning, while it was still dark, Jesus got up,
left the house and went off to a solitary place, where he prayed.
Simon and his companions went to look for him, and when
they found him, they exclaimed: "Everyone is looking for you!"
Jesus replied, "Let us go somewhere else—to the nearby villages—
so I can preach there also. That is why I have come."*

MARK 1:35-38

*A brother came to Scetis to visit Abba Moses and asked
him for a word. The old man said to him, "Go, sit in
your cell, and your cell will teach you everything."*

AS TOLD IN *THE SAYINGS OF THE DESERT FATHERS*

THE SECOND OLDEST of eight children, my mom, Nancy Arndt, grew up on a little family-owned farm in Auburndale, Wisconsin. Her parents, Richard and Delores Berdan, were as hard-working as they come, rising early and staying up late to make sure that everyone was provided for—no small feat, considering the size of the family.

As you might expect, everyone who was *provided for* also *contributed*. No one was exempt from the myriad tasks and responsibilities of running the farm. From tending to the cows to bailing hay to making sure that the fields were free of rocks—everyone had a hand in the daily labor.

My mom carried that kind of *rise-at-the-crack-of-dawn* work ethic well into her adult life. Indeed, she carried it into her spirituality. Some of my most vivid and enduring memories of my childhood involve wandering downstairs at 5 a.m. for a drink of water only to see my mom sitting at the island in the kitchen, poring over the Scriptures, pouring out her heart to God in fervent prayers muttered just under her breath. By that time, she'd generally already been at it for a half hour. She was just getting warmed up, just beginning to make her daily pilgrimage into the presence of God. Those words from the psalmist, "My soul followeth hard after thee" (Psalm 63:8, KJV)? That's my mom.

But she wasn't always that way. The faith of her childhood made little practical difference in her life until her mid-twenties, when she had a direct and personal encounter with Jesus. It changed everything. He became her love, her life. She sought him. He gave himself to her. Once she experienced the light and warmth of his presence, she made it her mission to keep returning to the source. Once, early on in their marriage, my dad went on a long hunting trip, and my mom decided to use the solitude for several days of fasting and prayer. Lost in prayer, she heard God speak:

He is the security you seek in money.
He is the high you seek in alcohol.
He is the ecstasy you seek in sex.
He is the health you seek in doctors.
He is the song you seek in music.
He is the dance you seek in nightclubs.
He is the beauty you seek in traveling.
He is the wisdom you seek in books.
He is the peace you seek in worry.
It is Jesus whom you seek.

The same God the psalmist knew: "With you is the fountain of life; in your light we see light" (Psalm 36:9); and Augustine knew: "Our souls are restless until they find rest in thee"; and Julian of Norwich knew: "No other heaven was pleasing to me than Jesus . . . my bliss"[1]—my mom was coming to know. *It is Jesus whom you seek.*

Her early mornings were a daily renewal of her quest to know the Lord. And it showed. Always warmth in her heart. Always wise words on her lips. Always an easy smile and a quick laugh. Always a peacemaking, reconciling presence. Always strength and more than enough strength for the tasks of life—strength that she shared with others.

My mom's way of life left a deep impression on me as a boy. Intuitively I grasped that the manner of her being—her strength, wisdom, and dignity—were connected in deep and indissoluble ways with her habit to seek the face of God before any of us were awake. She could be with us in ways that were healing because she was with God first. In his presence she daily let go of fear and anger and worry and regret to embrace the goodness of the Lord who is still making her a new creation (2 Corinthians 5:17). I saw then—and see now, even more clearly—that the manifest holiness and wholesomeness of her life and her daily spiritual practice were intimately connected.

As they are for all of us. If we seek to live into the Great Renunciation, we must develop some new habits.

ON FLEEING

One might argue that the defining feature of desert spirituality—or at least its most *obvious* feature—was the Desert Fathers' and Mothers' fanatical need to withdraw from human company to be with God.

In the late fourth century, a Roman aristocrat by the name of Arsenius sensed the call of the Lord to flee the trappings of status, money, and power in order to withdraw into the desert: "Abba Arsenius prayed to God in these words, 'Lord, lead me in the way of salvation.' And a voice came saying to him, 'Arsenius, flee from men and you will be saved.'"[2] Having done so, he placed himself under the direction of one of the most vibrant of the desert monks, Abba John the Dwarf.

Abba John understood the need to regularly withdraw:

> When [Abba John] returned from the harvest or when he
> had been with some of the old men, he gave himself to
> prayer, meditation and psalmody until his thoughts were
> re-established in their previous order.[3]

Prolonged exposure to people, John saw, had an inevitable disordering impact on the soul. If a person wanted to remain anchored in God, they would have to pull back from human company at frequent intervals to re-establish their "thoughts" in their previous order. Solitude and prayer, in other words, were essential habits of the desert.

The lesson seems not to have been lost on John's disciple Arsenius:

> Having withdrawn to the solitary life he made the same prayer again ["Lord, lead me in the way of salvation"] and he heard a voice saying to him, "Arsenius, flee, be silent, pray always, for these are the sources of sinlessness."[4]

The one-off withdrawal into the desert was not nearly enough to save Arsenius's life. Only by *regularly* engaging in the disciplines of solitude, silence, and prayer would Arsenius grow into holiness.

Everywhere you look in the desert tradition you see this. For the Desert Fathers and Mothers, holiness was not accidental. Nor did simply withdrawing to the desert ensure that they would find what they sought. No, holiness was a constant quest, a matter of daily habit. Sanctity was forged and continually rediscovered in the prayer closet. This is at the heart of what Abba Moses meant when he told the person asking him for a word to "go, sit in your cell, and your cell will teach you everything."[5] Or, as another anonymous figure from the desert put it, "A monk's cell is like the furnace in Babylon where the three young men found the Son of God. And it is like the pillar of cloud where God spoke to Moses."[6]

For the Desert Fathers and Mothers, the "cell"—that private

place of prayer—was not a place of religious tedium but rather a place of encounter with the Lord. A place where the Son of God could be discovered afresh in all his burning glory. Where God could speak as he spoke to Moses. A place of refreshing and renewal. And because it was so, they saw that withdrawal was crucial to a person's spiritual survival and flourishing. As Abba Anthony put it,

> Just as fish die if they stay too long out of water, so the
> monks who loiter outside their cells or pass their time
> with men of the world lose the intensity of inner peace.
> So like a fish going towards the sea, we must hurry to
> reach our cell, for fear that if we delay outside we will lose
> our interior watchfulness.[7]

THE ART OF WITHDRAWAL

In their withdrawal, the Desert Fathers and Mothers were patterning themselves after Jesus. When you look at the life of Jesus in the Gospels, one of the things that immediately strikes you is his habit of withdrawing both from his disciples and from the crowds to seek the face of God. According to the witness of the Gospel writers, that habit seems to have been a profound source of strength and clarity for him:

> Very early in the morning, while it was still dark, Jesus
> got up, left the house and went off to a solitary place,
> where he prayed. Simon and his companions went to
> look for him, and when they found him, they exclaimed:
> "Everyone is looking for you!"

Jesus replied, "Let us go somewhere else—to the
nearby villages—so I can preach there also. That is why I
have come."

MARK 1:35-38

Once it begins, the ministry of Jesus accelerates quickly in the
Gospels. He is baptized, then tempted in the desert, and then
enormous crowds appear—men and women and children hanging
on his every deed and word, pressing in on him for healing and
deliverance and wisdom about the Kingdom.

And so Jesus gets up "very early in the morning, while it was
still dark" and heads out to what Mark calls "a solitary place" so
that he could pray. When Simon and the other disciples find him,
they express some measure of exasperation: *Jesus! What are you
doing here? The movement is underway, and you are the star of the
show. Everyone is looking for you. They need you. You have responsibilities and obligations. This is no time to run away. You need to be
present to keep the momentum going!*

And Jesus does something stunning. He tells Simon that it
is time to leave—whatever momentum they have in that area
notwithstanding—and preach the gospel "somewhere else,"
because "that is why I have come." Jesus' mind is profoundly clear.
He refuses to get caught up in the hysteria of his emerging celebrity. Instead, he perceives the voice of God underneath the noise
of the moment and declares that it is time to move on.

The Old Testament scholar Walter Brueggemann once said
that if pastors want to fulfill their calling to bring "a word from
elsewhere," they would have to "live . . . from elsewhere."[8] No one
embodied this better than Jesus. His habit of withdrawing from

the noise of the crowds and the clamor of his disciples, consistently turning to prayer and intimate communion with the Father, anchored him in another reality: the truest, most real reality—the very will of God. Because he lived *elsewhere*, he was free even from his own success to hear and respond to the voice of the Father. He could cut through the illusions and pretensions and demands of people in order to yield himself fully to the will of his Father. *That is why I have come.*

To add a bit more depth to the picture, the word that Mark uses in this text to designate Jesus' place of prayer—*erēmos*—is the very same word he used to designate the location of Jesus' temptation in verse 12: namely, the wilderness. The same place where Jesus, for forty days, fasted and prayed, doing battle with the devil, being ministered to by angels, and coming forth with strength and clarity of purpose for the mission *was the place where he regularly withdrew to renew his strength and clarity of purpose for the mission.*

Jesus' life continued to be marked by frequent and regular moments of withdrawing from people in order to renew his communion with the Father, his sense of what the Father was calling him to do and be. Jesus knew how to find strength, clarity, and resolve in the presence of God.

Many of the most pivotal moments in the Gospels take place in and around moments like these. The choosing of the Twelve. John the Baptist's death. Jesus' teaching on the Lord's Prayer. His agony and bloody sweat in Gethsemane on the night he was handed over to suffering and death. Luke remarks that, following Jesus' forty days in the wilderness, he "returned to Galilee in the power of the Spirit" (Luke 4:14). I think that serves as a description of *every* time Jesus withdrew to the wilderness for prayer: He emerged from it in the power of the Spirit.

THE FURNACE OF TRANSFORMATION

One of foundational realities of the Christian faith is that Jesus is both fully (and truly) God and fully (and truly) human. So not only does Jesus—by his life, death, and resurrection—show us what it means to be *God*; but he also, as the Son of God made human, *shows us what it means to be human*. We cannot and will not be fully human until we are human as Jesus is human,[9] which is exactly what the Desert Fathers and Mothers are trying to teach us when it comes to solitude and prayer: When we withdraw into the wilderness, as Jesus did, to seek fellowship with God, we become more fully who we were and are created to be.

But just what is it about the withdrawal into the wilderness, into the "cell," that does this for us?

Over forty years ago, Henri Nouwen observed that "our society is not a community radiant with the love of Christ, but a dangerous network of domination and manipulation in which we can easily get entangled and lose our soul." Nouwen goes on to wonder aloud if we "have not already been so deeply molded by the seductive powers of our dark world that we have become blind to our own and other people's fatal state and have lost the power and motivation to swim for our lives."[10]

And this is easy enough to see in our present day, isn't it? When I read Nouwen's words, I immediately began to think about what social media has become in our time. Back in 2006 and 2007, when platforms like Facebook and Twitter were just finding their footing, the medium was fun and engaging and fresh—status updates and #hashtagging, sharing content you found funny or meaningful, connecting with friends new and old. The democratizing effect of it was just so energizing. People that you'd never have a chance to connect with in normal life suddenly became available to you with a simple click of the button. (I'll never forget the day when a friend of mine and I tweeted at the actor Carl Weathers—Apollo Creed of *Rocky* fame—on his birthday, *and he actually responded!* What a beautiful new world!)

But years later, we have learned, tragically, that the same power—to connect, to share ideas and shape thoughts, to build up and bless—can also be and is often used to tear down, overthrow, and destroy. Social media quickly amplifies the insanity of our times. Groupthink is a constant threat. The outrage machine churns day and night. The threat of being "canceled" looms ever over our heads. How will we keep from losing our footing? How will we escape the many threats and temptations of our day?

Only by doing as Jesus did, and the fathers and mothers of the desert after him: by withdrawing regularly into the wilderness of solitude and prayer to rediscover God—and ourselves—and to be transformed in the process. Nouwen comments:

> Solitude is the furnace of transformation. Without
> solitude we remain victims of our society and continue to
> be entangled in the illusions of the false self. Jesus himself
> entered into this furnace. There he was tempted with
> the three compulsions of the world: to be relevant ("turn
> stones into loaves"), to be spectacular ("throw yourself
> down"), and to be powerful ("I will give you all these
> kingdoms"). There he affirmed God as the only source of
> his identity ("You must worship the Lord your God and
> serve him alone") [Matthew 4:1-11]. Solitude is the place
> of the great struggle and the great encounter—the struggle
> against the compulsions of the false self and the encounter

with the loving God who offers himself as the substance of
the new self.[11]

This strikes right to the heart of the matter. It also helps us
understand just what is at stake in the call to regularly withdraw
into the "furnace" of one's cell. A conversation between some
monks and Abba Agathon helps us see it with even more clarity:

> The brethren also asked him, "Amongst all good works,
> which is the virtue which requires the greatest effort?"
> He answered, "Forgive me, but I think there is no labor
> greater than that of prayer to God. For every time a man
> wants to pray, his enemies, the demons, want to prevent
> him, for they know that it is only by turning him from
> prayer that they can hinder his journey. Whatever good
> work a man undertakes, if he perseveres in it, he will
> attain rest. But prayer is warfare to the last breath."[12]

I have been following Jesus all my life, and I know something
now that I did not know in my early years: As you progress in the
spiritual life, the stakes only get higher. As you advance in your
career, as people in the community of faith come to depend on
you, as your children grow, as your wealth and power increase, so
also do the measure of temptation and the demand on your spiritual life increase. Not only that, but I am now firmly convinced
that the further into this you go, the more aware you become of
your own humanness; that is, your own capacity for self-deception,
your own predilection to folly.

And so where you had hoped that perhaps prayer would

function in your life as a sort of rest and retreat, you instead see that withdrawal into the wilderness for prayer is a daily, urgent necessity; indeed, it is a "warfare to the last breath." Prayer is a place where we wrestle with demons, with ourselves, and finally, with God. In the struggle, like the patriarch Jacob, we are changed, becoming in the process creatures who better reflect the glory of God, creatures who are more capable of love.

It is the orientation to God and to others that gives the desert call to withdraw its distinctive character. Abba Theodore of Pherme said that "the man who has learnt the sweetness of the cell flees from his neighbor *but not as though he despised him.*"[13] Sometimes the way you hear Christians talk about solitude makes it seem as though the "cell" is a provision of the Lord to get away from—yuck—*people*. But that is wrong, for it defies the very nature of the salvation that we have been called into. God does not save us *from* people but *for* people and *into a people*—the church (more on this in part two). *People are the entire point of the work of God in Christ*, and if our spirituality is going to be deserving of the name *Christian*, then it will and must be oriented to people.

The *point*, in other words, of the withdrawal into solitude and prayer is not contempt for or frustration with others (though, make no mistake, quite often frustration in community life—which has as much to do with ourselves as with others—will push us into the wilderness) but, rather, the desire to be ordered to them rightly.

THE DAY WITH OTHERS, THE DAY ALONE

Relationships are at the heart of desert spirituality. Rowan Williams remarks that in "fleeing" from time to time the company of others, the Desert Fathers and Mothers were "entering into a more serious level of responsibility for themselves and others" and that "their relationships were essential to the understanding of their vocation."[14]

As with them, so with us. When God calls us, he calls us into relationship. That is foundational to the entire perspective of Scripture. And his constant call to us is to be sanctified *so that* we can be in relationship with others rightly. I cannot be the husband I need to be to Mandi; the father I need to be to Ethan, Gabe, Bella, and Liam; the friend I need to be to my loved ones; the colleague I need to be to my coworkers; or the pastor I need to be to the congregation I serve unless I regularly and frequently head to the wilderness to wrestle with myself, with the encroaching darkness, and even, at times, with the Lord who loves and calls me. I think often of Paul's words to Timothy—"Watch your life and doctrine closely. Persevere in them, because if you do, you will save both yourself and your hearers" (1 Timothy 4:16)—and of Jesus' words in his high priestly prayer—"For them I sanctify myself, that they too may be truly sanctified" (John 17:19). According to the witness of Scripture, the end goal of our sanctification is that we would be sanctified and sanctifying gifts for other people.[15]

By the same token, the whole point of withdrawing into solitude and prayer is to have all that spoils the divine image in us (and therefore in community life)—anger and fear and self-righteousness—burned away in the presence of God, so that we can be in the body of Christ for the sake of the world the way the Lord would have us be. That is what prayer is all about. As we have heard Abba Nilus say before, "Prayer is the seed of gentleness and the absence of anger." We go to the prayer closet to be made new creations who can be present in the body of Christ and present in the world as the Lord would have us—gently and without anger, redemptively and transformatively.

The dynamic of solitude and community is a distinctive mark of Christian spirituality, one brilliantly captured by Dietrich Bonhoeffer in *Life Together*. Bonhoeffer wrote this now-classic work during his time leading the illegal preachers' seminaries at Zingst and Finkenwalde, where he and a small group of seminarians lived together and trained for the work of preaching in the Confessing Church during the rise of the Third Reich.

After outlining his vision for the indispensability of community for the life of faith ("Christianity means community through Jesus Christ and in Jesus Christ"[16]), Bonhoeffer goes on to characterize the dynamic between togetherness and apartness as "The Day with Others" and "The Day Alone." I'll have more to say on his thoughts about "The Day with Others" in subsequent chapters, but for our purposes here I want you to pay close attention to what he says about the need to be alone:

> Many people seek fellowship because they are afraid to be alone. Because they cannot stand loneliness, they are driven to seek the company of other people. . . . The person who comes into a fellowship because he is running away from himself is misusing it for the sake of diversion, no matter how spiritual this diversion may appear. He is really not seeking community at all, but only distraction which will allow him to forget his loneliness for a brief time, the very alienation that creates the deadly isolation of man.[17]

Bonhoeffer minces no words here—and draws attention to a core pathology that human beings have likely been dealing with since the dawn of the species: namely, that because of our fear and discomfort with our disordered interior lives, and in a perverse effort to flee from that disorder, we seek solace in the company of others. Rather than dealing with what is going on inside, we look for cheap consolation in community. But when we engage community without dealing with our interior disorder, we will eventually discover that even community cannot shelter us from ourselves. Our disorder will find us there, too. Which is why five centuries earlier, the German-Dutch monk Thomas à Kempis (himself reflecting on the witness of the desert) remarked that "the only man who can safely appear in public is the one who wishes he were at home."[18]

Bonhoeffer keenly observes that the person who runs to community for cheap consolation is "generally disappointed," which disappointment is followed by their turning around and "blam[ing] the fellowship for what is really their own fault."[19] And now judgment has been loosed into the community, which never ends well.

Fellowship is spoiled, Bonhoeffer thinks, when we use it to run from our issues. Which is why he says, "*Let him who cannot be alone beware of community*. He will only do harm to himself and to the community."[20] But then—and here's the brilliance of Bonhoeffer's vision—he goes on to say that "the reverse is also true: *Let him who is not in community beware of being alone*. Into the community you were called, the call was not meant for you alone; in the community of the called you bear your cross, you struggle, you pray." He continues:

You are not alone, even in death, and on the Last Day you will be only one member of the great congregation of Jesus Christ. If you scorn the fellowship of the brethren, you reject the call of Jesus Christ, and thus your solitude can only be hurtful to you. . . .

We recognize, then, that only as we are within the fellowship can we be alone, and only he that is alone can live in the fellowship. Only in the fellowship do we learn to be rightly alone and only in aloneness do we learn to live rightly in the fellowship. It is not as though the one preceded the other; both begin at the same time, namely, with the call of Jesus Christ.[21]

So on the one hand, the only way to escape the illusions of community and society is by regularly withdrawing from them—and on the other, the only way to prevent retreats into solitude, silence, and prayer from devolving into self-congratulatory nonsense is by remembering that the Christ we seek to encounter also calls us into his body and shapes us daily to be holy members of it.

It has taken me, frankly, a long time to understand this. I am an introvert and something of a mystic by nature. I love people and I love my friends, but if you give me the choice to spend time with people or to spend time alone, I am choosing "alone"—every time. Time alone with God, with a book, on the porch, by myself, on a long walk, drinking in the sights and sounds of nature or listening to good music, praying and pondering, musing on a potential poem or writing the next essay or chapter to a book or thinking through a coming sermon—that's my favorite place to be.

And what I have to remember—constantly—is that the Lord in his mercy *grants* me those places of solitude not just to renew my own connection with him *but also and equally as importantly* to purify and strengthen me in my service to my family, to the church, and to the world. I don't get to run into solitude with eyes and ears covered, pretending that the world beyond me doesn't exist. No, it is *this world* into which Christ came; *this world* on behalf of which he bled and died; *this world* for which he is calling, forming, and sending his body—and me as a part of it. Mother Teresa said it so well in a little aphorism printed on the back of her business card:

> *The fruit of silence is prayer.*
> *The fruit of prayer is faith.*
> *The fruit of faith is love.*
> *The fruit of love is service.*
> *The fruit of service is peace.*[22]

The call into solitude for me must be a place of sanctification for vocation—for the unique and varied ways that the Lord calls me into the company of others. The *reason* that I, like my mom (and dad—another notoriously early riser who daily brought himself before the face of God) before me, rise early to be still in God's presence;

the *reason* that I, in the middle of a busy day, will often head out for a quick walk on the trail behind my house to recollect my mind and heart and reposition myself for the remainder of the day's tasks and challenges;

the *reason* that I, at the end of the day, get quiet to ask forgiveness and release the burdens of the day before I head into the darkness of sleep;

the *reason* that I, several times throughout the year, withdraw by myself for solitude retreats—

is *so that* I can be the person God has called me to be, in the right way, with others.

Which is precisely what the Desert Fathers and Mothers were getting at. "A monk's cell is like . . . the pillar of cloud where God spoke to Moses." And the same God who called Moses into his vocation *among the people* calls us to bear the cross *in the service of others.*

A BASIC TEMPLATE

One of the things that has astonished me over the years is that no matter how widely you read across the centuries, the basic forms of daily Christian spirituality remain largely the same. So how should a person approach the daily retreat into "the wilderness"? Here are a few pointers, which the Desert Fathers and Mothers would heartily recommend.

First, find a consistent time and place to withdraw. For most people, the morning is best—before the rush of the day hits. For others, it is sometime in the middle of the day. And for still others, evening is best—when the dust has settled. (And some do all three!) Pick what works for you and stick to it. (The advantage of the morning is that it helps you find sure footing before you head into your day.)

Second, make sure the place is comfortable and quiet. A room of the house with a comfortable chair and soft light will do just fine. Find a place where you can easily center down into God's presence.

Third, when you get there, take a few moments to become still. My worst devotional times are the ones I rush into and rush through. We need to ready ourselves to enter God's presence. So take some time to become quiet. A few deep breaths will help. Release whatever you're carrying, and ask God to help you become openhearted, receptive, and attentive.

Fourth, make the Scripture the centerpiece of your time alone. Augustine said, "For now treat the Scripture of God as the face of

God. Melt in its presence."[23] Do that. Approach the Scriptures as a search for the face of God. Or as a feast that the Lord has set before you. Chew slowly and savor what you eat. Let the Lord nourish you by it. Often, as you are reading Scripture, you'll be provoked to repent of something. Repent of it! Or you'll be reminded of a situation you've been worrying about. Pray over it! Or you'll be given insight into a problem that you've been seeking a solution for. Thank God for it! The Scriptures, never forget, are the light of the Light of God to us—Jesus is lighting our path by them. They are the word of the Word of God to us—Jesus is speaking to us in them. They are the bread of the Bread of Life to us—Jesus is feeding us by them. Receive them as such.

Fifth, when you have concluded your reading of Scripture, present your requests for the day to God. Lay them out in his presence and ask that light and grace fall upon them all. Pray over those whose lives intertwine with your own—family, friends, neighbors, church. I often use the Lord's Prayer as a template during this time—it helps me articulate my concerns for myself and others in a "Kingdom" register.

Finally, be still and wait on the Lord. Breathe deeply of his presence. Listen for the Lord's direction on places where you are confused or seeking wisdom. See how the strong shoulders of the Resurrected One are sufficient to carry all you are concerned about. Take up the easy yoke of trust again. Receive the Spirit afresh.

Then go into your day with strength and joy, knowing that the Presence goes with you in the coming hours.

PART TWO

INTO THE DESERT WITH OTHERS

Here the essential context of the holy life

comes into view: namely, the church.

No genuine Christian spirituality grows up without it.

As we ponder the witness of

the Desert Fathers and Mothers,

let us hear their call to community—

which is at once a rebuke to

every self-directed spirituality

and a discovery of the redemptive mystery

God enfleshes in the church.

CHAPTER 4

CALLED TO COMMUNITY

The Peril of Self-Directed Spirituality

We were all baptized by one Spirit so as to form one body—whether Jews or Gentiles, slave or free—and we were all given the one Spirit to drink.
1 CORINTHIANS 12:13

For withdrawal into total solitude was found to lead to moral collapse, mental eccentricity, even to madness. The hermit was one of a company of hermits, who lived under a common discipline with a superior; who said their allotted psalms, each in his cell, at common times each day; who met on Sundays at least, sometimes on Saturdays as well, for common worship and a common meal and a discussion of the spiritual life.
OWEN CHADWICK

My FIRST JOB after seminary was as an associate pastor at a church in Oklahoma. The church, at several hundred members, was only a few years old, and the senior/planting pastor was looking to hire a kind of jack-of-all-trades associate to help with preaching, worship planning, outreach, pastoral care, and community development (classes, small groups, etc.). It was a good job for a twenty-five-year-old fresh out of seminary, and I attacked it with eagerness.

That last part of the assignment was what led me into friendship with Tim. Tim and his wife, Sarah, were in their fifties and had been Christians for most of their adult lives, serving in a number of churches as leaders in a variety of capacities.[1]

Most recently, before attending our church, Tim and Sarah had been church planters. Over the years, Tim—while not a pastor by occupation—had proven to be a gifted communicator and pastoral presence. When the Sunday school class he led at a previous church swelled to more than two hundred people in weekly attendance, the leadership of that church—in an effort to run with what it seemed like the Spirit was so evidently doing—decided to send Tim and Sarah out to plant. And so out they went, with people and resources and great eagerness.

The plant did not go well. Somehow, in the transition from Sunday school to church, the community lost its magic. The initial burst of excitement didn't amount to anything. Before long, attendance and giving slowly dwindled until finally, just two painful years in, Tim and Sarah decided to raise the white flag and walk away.

The experience left Tim eviscerated. "On paper" the plant had all it needed: communal discernment, appropriately vetted leadership, a vibrant core, resources, and covering. Plus, Tim and Sarah—so far as they knew—hadn't engaged the effort with selfish motives. Clean hands and pure hearts. You could hardly ask for a better setup. And still, it failed.

For Tim, the failure of the plant affected him in two ways. First, it made him cautious with respect to the church. *Stay involved, but keep it at arm's length. You don't want to get burned again.* Second, it made him—in his own words—"polite" in his relationship with God. *I could never deny you. But I'm not sure I can trust you like that again.* In short, Tim became guarded. A winter chill settled over his once trusting and indefatigably warm heart.

Despite all of that, Tim and I enjoyed a growing friendship. When I decided to launch an experimental "formation group" one fall, Tim was at the top of my list of people to invite to join. The goal of the group was simple: gather each week to talk about (a) what we were struggling with in our lives, (b) what we were hearing God saying in and over the struggle, and (c) how we sensed him asking us to respond. My hope was that in creating a structured space of straightforward honesty, we would see the Spirit move in all our lives.

Happily, Tim—along with a handful of others—said yes. Week after week we met, discussing life's struggles, discerning the voice of the Spirit, learning to yield and follow. It became the highlight of the week for each of us, learning each other's stories and watching redemption unfold—mostly in small ways, sometimes in large ways—right in front of our eyes.

One week I decided to do a kind of check-in with everyone— what the experience had been like for them so far. We went around the circle and shared. When it came to Tim, his words left me speechless:

When I joined this group, truthfully, I was really skeptical. I've done this kind of thing before, and I didn't have a lot of hope that anything would happen. But it seemed fun, and I like you guys, so I joined. You all know what we've been through. I would never walk away from God, but our experience with the church plant left me cold inside. Cold to the church, cold toward God. But something is changing in me. I'm not sure how it's happening; I just know that it is. Something about coming here, week after week, getting to know you guys and opening my own heart, letting you speak into and over me . . . warmth is coming back in, the ice is thawing.

He ended with this line:

"I can *feel* again."

Within a year of that moment, Tim and Sarah had risen in our midst as vibrant leaders, serving in the full range of their gifts with joy and strength—leading seminars and groups, mentoring and coaching, blessing everyone who had the good fortune of interacting with them. It was a wonder to behold.

CALLED TO COMMUNITY

Bill was being transformed by the power of the Spirit, mediated through a vital relationship with the community of faith. The church, according to the witness of Old and New Testaments alike, is the foundational and indispensable context for the flourishing of human life.

You'll notice that I didn't say "spiritual" life. Too often, our sense of the importance of the community of faith boils down to something we vaguely call "spirituality"—the invisible, interior part of ourselves that has little to do with our actual lives. Church, we think, is about *that*.

But that perspective is foreign to the Scriptures. Belonging to the community of faith is not about helping you cultivate a private interiority or personal sense of the transcendent but about bringing rectitude to your whole life—spirit, mind, and body. The church is God's answer to the calamity of Eden.

The Bible's witness to this is set out early in Scripture. Following the expulsion from the Garden, the brutal murder of Cain by Abel, the devastation of the Flood, and the scattering of humanity at the tower of Babel, we read this in Genesis 12:

> The LORD had said to Abram, "Go from your country,
> your people and your father's household to the land I will
> show you.
>
> "I will make you into a great nation,
>   and I will bless you;
> I will make your name great,
>   and you will be a blessing.
> I will bless those who bless you,
>   and whoever curses you I will curse;
> and all peoples on earth
>   will be blessed through you."
>
> GENESIS 12:1-3

Now the word *bless* or *blessing* perhaps does not mean very much to you, but to the ears of ancient Hebrews, it meant an enormous amount. One Hebrew dictionary describes the meaning of the word *bless* (Hebrew: *bārak* as "to endue someone with special power."[2] That is why you see the word used in the Creation story of Genesis 1 and 2 (*of the animals*—1:22; *of humans*—1:28; *of the Sabbath*—2:3) and also throughout the Pentateuch as a description of *what happens when* the people of God decide to walk in obedience to his commands; namely, that God's power is released over their lives (e.g., *of food*: Exodus 23:25; *of the fruit of the womb and the ground*: Deuteronomy 7:13; *of the work of their hands*: Deuteronomy 28:12).

Here's how the Old Testament scholar Walter Brueggemann describes the word *bārak*:

> A blessing is an act—by speech or gesture—whereby one party transmits power for life to another party. . . .
> God . . . is the primal speaker and giver of blessing.[3]

So when we come to Genesis 12 and see that God has placed his "blessing" upon this *family*, this *community*, our ears should perk up because the writer of Genesis is setting the agenda for the rest of the Scriptures: *A community will be the carrier of the life and vitality of God down through the centuries.*

Brueggemann goes on to remark that "while God's power for life is given directly in God's utterance, human agents . . . can also mediate a blessing." That is what Abraham and his family, which later grew into what we know as the nation of Israel, are: God's community that mediates the blessing of life to the world; God's solution to the calamity of Eden. They are the objects and subjects of the Lord's gracious, life-giving, life-restoring *bārak*.

That's why the priests of the Old Testament were commanded to speak over the people as they did:

The LORD said to Moses, "Tell Aaron and his sons, 'This
is how you are to bless the Israelites. Say to them:

"The LORD bless you
    and keep you;
the LORD make his face shine on you
    and be gracious to you;
the LORD turn his face toward you
    and give you peace.'"

"So they will put my name on the Israelites, and I will
bless them."

NUMBERS 6:22-27

That sense of blessing as power for life is not diminished but
intensified as we come to the New Testament. Jesus, as the one
whose death takes the curse for us (Galatians 3:13) blesses his
community from and with his resurrected life:

When he had led them out to the vicinity of Bethany,
he lifted up his hands and blessed them. While he was
blessing them, he left them and was taken up into heaven.
Then they worshiped him and returned to Jerusalem
with great joy. And they stayed continually at the temple,
praising God.

LUKE 24:50-53

Great joy, praise, and—later on, as we learn in the book of
Acts—power for mission come to the community of faith from
the intensified blessing of the Great High Priest, Jesus the Lord.

That power and blessing continue to work in and through the church:

> I pray that the eyes of your heart may be enlightened in order that you may know the hope to which he has called you, the riches of his glorious inheritance in his holy people, and his incomparably great power for us who believe. That power is the same as the mighty strength he exerted when he raised Christ from the dead and seated him at his right hand in the heavenly realms, far above all rule and authority, power and dominion, and every name that is invoked, not only in the present age but also in the one to come. And God placed all things under his feet and appointed him to be head over everything for the church, which is his body, the fullness of him who fills everything in every way.
>
> EPHESIANS 1:18-23

We could multiply references from the New Testament, but the point in any case would remain clear—the church is the location where the promise given to Abraham finds fulfillment. *This community* is the carrier of the world-redeeming, cosmos-renewing, human-life-restoring power of God. We will not find God—or, by the same token, ourselves—apart from this community.

THE DESERT'S WITNESS TO COMMUNITY

This puts in perspective what Dietrich Bonhoeffer was driving at when he said that while the person who cannot be alone should beware of community, on the other hand, "Let him who is not in community beware of being alone." *Beware* is a very strong word. Why would he say that?

Bonhoeffer was profoundly aware, as the Desert Fathers and Mothers were before him, that God has made us for fellowship. We cannot be all that we have been called to be—we cannot be truly human—until we have embraced the call to community.

Now that may seem at least a bit *odd* to our ears, since our notion of the Desert Fathers and Mothers is generally of a group of people who radically rejected the company of others in order to seek God in the quiet chambers of their hearts. While it certainly *was* true that they tended to be cautious of the danger of over-exposure to people, at the same time they knew that they *needed* others—that there was (and is) no salvation apart from the community of faith.

The early church had a saying: *extra ecclesium nulla salus*— "outside of the church there is no salvation." British professor of church history Owen Chadwick puts what they meant by that in bold relief:

> For withdrawal into total solitude was found to lead to moral collapse, mental eccentricity, even to madness. The hermit was one of a company of hermits, who lived under a common discipline with a superior; who said their allotted psalms, each in his cell, at common times each day; who met on Sundays at least, sometimes on Saturdays as well, for common worship and a common meal and a discussion of the spiritual life.[4]

No matter how much the Desert Fathers and Mothers emphasized the value of "apartness" for the life of faith, at their best they assumed that such apartness could only exist *inside* a delicate and well-balanced ecosystem of community. No one should be alone (to use Bonhoeffer's word) unless they situated that aloneness in the context of a constellation of relationships: with a spiritual director, with the worshiping community, and with peers with whom they shared meals and discussed the spiritual life. Failing to engage community in that way, Chadwick says, led to a kind of disintegration: "moral collapse, mental eccentricity, even to madness."[5]

And the stories are there to back it up. Let's return to John Cassian and Germanus for a moment. In the second of their conversations with Abba Moses, Moses begins to spell out the importance of community for the life of faith but approaches it by way of the concept of *discernment*:

> If a monk does not do his utmost to acquire
> [discernment] and if he does not have a clear knowledge
> of the spirits rising up against him he will surely stray
> like someone in a dark night amid gruesome shadows
> and not only will he stumble into dangerous pits and
> down steep slopes but he will often fall even in the level,
> straightforward places.[6]

As an example, Moses tells Cassian and Germanus about a monk by the name of Hero who had lived fifty years in more or less complete isolation. The rigor of his spiritual life and severity of his self-denial were widely known. And yet, a snake lurked in the grass of his spirituality—a delusion that would finally lead to his undoing. Moses notes that "he preferred to be guided by his own ideas rather than to bow to the advice and conferences of his brethren and to the rules laid down by our predecessors."[7]

As the years went on, in other words, Hero's spirituality became completely self-directed. Subject to nothing and no one but his own idea of what was good and right, Hero unwittingly fell prey to that which Christianity has classically thought of as the mother of all sins: pride. Thinking himself better than others, Hero shut out the wisdom of community and therefore—just to the same extent—the wisdom of God. His very humanity was undone by his increasing separation from the church.

Towards the end, he could not even be persuaded to join the brethren for worship and a meal on Easter Sunday, preferring—the absurdity should be evident by now—to commune with the God who raised Jesus from the dead *apart from* the community that is the direct result, impact, and carrier of his resurrection life. For Moses, the result of this demonic delusion was as tragic as it was predictable:

> This presumptuousness led to his being fooled. He showed the utmost veneration for the angel of Satan, welcoming him as if he were actually an angel of light. Yielding totally to his bondage he threw himself headlong into a well, whose depths no eye could penetrate. He did so trusting completely in the assurance of the angel who had guaranteed that on account of the merit of his virtues and of his works he could never come to any harm. To experience his undoubted freedom from danger the deluded man threw himself in the darkness of night into this well. He would know at first hand the great merit of his own virtue when he emerged unscathed. He was pulled out half-dead by his brothers, who had to struggle very hard at it. He would die two days later. Worse, he

was to cling firmly to his illusion, and the very experience of dying could not persuade him that he had been the sport of devilish skill.[8]

THE PROBLEM IN OUR DAY

How many people can you think of in your own life whose presumptuous pride led to calamity? I'm willing to bet that as you read these words, half a dozen people or more immediately come to mind. Folks who were once in vital community all of a sudden thought they knew better, separated themselves from the church, and came to disaster. It is one of the commonest and saddest perils of the spiritual life and—beware—becomes an ever-greater "occupational hazard" as you mature. If you're not careful, you'll start believing that you're better than others; that you don't need the pesky and sometimes irritating "communion of saints" speaking into your life anymore; that you are above the counsel, direction, rebuke, and correction of the folks you are in community with. Right there, with the onset of that belief, you court disaster.

As a pastor and lifelong member of the church, I've seen it over and over. Kids who grew up in church who came of age and decided to throw their faith away. Spouses who decided that the marriage vow they made in the sight of God and "all these witnesses" was just too difficult and constricting and that they'd be better off if they were free to discover themselves. Mature saints who one day decided that the dogmas of the church were just too restrictive, and they'd like to try their hand at a kind of do-it-yourself spirituality. Even pastors and teachers who after years of preaching and teaching started feeling like they knew better and decided to cut bait with the historic faith of the church in favor of being self-styled spiritual gurus, motivational speakers, or life coaches—preferring (to use Moses' words) "to be guided by [their] own ideas rather than to bow to the advice and conferences of [their] brethren and to the rules laid down by our predecessors."

Now, in perfect honesty, I get why many people do this. I think there's a narrowness and rigidity, suffocating and unhelpful, that often masquerades in the church as faithfulness. I've sat with dozens, maybe hundreds, of kids in their teens and twenties who told me they were losing their faith and on the verge of walking away from church, and when I probed more deeply, I found that the "faith" they were losing was a faith where you couldn't question how old the earth was or read or watch *Harry Potter* or wonder too loudly whether Hindus who never really heard the gospel would wind up in the Kingdom. Similarly, I've sat with many spouses over the years who were *this close* to throwing their marriages away, and when we got down to what was really going on, they simply needed a space where they could tell the truth about the deep fears and desires they were afraid to voice because they weren't sure how those things would be received. Likewise, I've sat with mature saints who stood on the very brink of abandoning their faith because of questions and doubts they feared were fatal only to discover (to their great relief) that they were simply giving voice to the kinds of courageous questions the faithful have been asking for two thousand years—and just didn't know it because no one had ever told them. Fundamentalism, I'm tempted to say, has shipwrecked more lives than secularism ever dreamed of.

Which goes back to why we need community. But not just any kind of community. We need wise, thoughtful, deep, honest community. Community that can hold the emerging faith of young adults, the many difficulties associated with marriage and family and work, the doubts and questions of the saints as they arise and

STREAMS IN THE WASTELAND

as they (often) become more pronounced over the years—without hitting the panic button. Community that offers an open heart, a listening ear, and wise counsel (where called for). Community where generous, ongoing friendship is possible because we know that Jesus is Lord over peoples' lives and stories—and that because nothing that is genuinely human frightens him, it should not frighten us either.

Years ago, when I was pastoring in Denver, my friend Steve—married, father of two, and a longtime, faithful follower of Jesus—witnessed a horrible and senseless tragedy. A homeless man panhandling at an intersection where Steve was waiting for the light to change tripped and fell under the wheel of an eighteen-wheeler. The man was instantly killed, and Steve, who was a primary witness, had to stay for several hours while first responders sorted out the mess.

The tragedy shook him to the core. I remember sitting with Steve at an IHOP one morning, discussing what had happened and trying together to make sense of it all. For Steve, it wasn't just the understandable trauma of witnessing something so gruesome. It was the theological questions that really shook him. *How could this happen? Where was God in that? What was/is the meaning of that man's life?* For Steve, it was difficult to ascribe *any* meaning to *anything* after witnessing such a tragedy.

That morning, over pancakes and coffee, I offered Steve the best gift I think we can give anyone—the gift of presence. I said to him, "Steve, I don't think I can offer you any theological perspective that will even remotely satisfy your questions. I think the questions are too deep, and too burning, for my words to do any good. I think the Lord is going to have to meet you in the questions. But I can offer you this—I can and will be a friend to you through this, whatever you need. And I am 100 percent confident that you are going to come out of it okay. And not just okay. But better than you were before."

A week later, Steve along with his wife, Suzy, and I went up to the intersection where the homeless man had been killed and conducted a little memorial service together. Just the three of us. We acknowledged the price that the Lord Jesus had paid for the man's life. That he was infinitely precious to God. That while we did not understand what happened, we were trusting God to hold not only his life but our own hurting, confused lives and hearts with mercy and understanding. And we spoke the Name—Father, Son, and Holy Spirit—over that corner, pleading that blessing would be released where the unthinkable had occurred. In our eyes, at least, that pavement once defiled by a senseless tragedy had become holy ground.

Many months later, while we were preparing to transition from the church in Denver to our new assignment in Colorado Springs, Steve wrote me a note: "I will never forget the way you entered into my pain. You looked me in the eye and told me that I would be okay. I didn't believe you at the time. But you were right. That was a lifeline for me. From the bottom of my heart—thank you."

ON "DISCERNMENT"

The Desert Fathers and Mothers would have called my conversation with Steve "discernment"—the ability to hold the complexities of life within an atmosphere of patient wisdom as we wait for God's salvation to unfold. Moses said to Cassian and Germanus that

> no virtue can come to full term or can endure without the grace of discernment. . . . It is discernment which with

firm step leads the enduring monk to God. . . . With discernment it is possible to reach the utmost heights with the minimum of exhaustion. Without it there are many who despite the intensity of their struggle have been quite unable to arrive at the summit of perfection. For discernment is the mother, the guardian, and the guide of all the virtues.[9]

What a remark. Only when we experience the wisdom of community do we reach the summit of perfection held out to us as the goal of the spiritual life.

One of the curiosities of our day is the staggering naiveté we bring to conversations and questions surrounding the most important matters of life. To become a lawyer, doctor, or scientist, a person must spend many years in training, submitting their minds and bodies to the wisdom of those who have gone before them, habituating themselves to the realities of their subject matter. But for some reason, when it comes to the very important questions—"Who are we? What are we made for? What does it mean to have a soul, how does it work, and what ruins and redeems it?"—we have an inbuilt assumption that one person's ideas about those questions are as good as the next, and that no one has a right to criticize anyone else's thoughts about the matter.

I can only conclude that we either think that those questions are *purely* subjective and have no essential bearing on *what's really real*, or we're just foolish enough to prioritize some vague idea of "tolerance" over our desperate thirst for genuine wisdom. Either way, it takes a pretty sturdy and ongoing denial of reality to fail to realize that the questions really *do* matter. As nice as the idea that no one has the right to criticize anyone else is, when push comes to shove, *we need wisdom,* and some notions of what is good and right for our humanity are better than others. When I'm under the knife for heart surgery, I don't want my doctor saying that "all roads lead to successful heart surgeries." I want her saying, "I've studied and trained, and, in my considered judgment, the path we are about to take is the best path I know of. You can trust me." We are not relativists about things that really matter.

Part of what Christianity offers is a several-thousand-year-old ongoing reflection on the deepest and most vexing questions facing humanity. It assumes that we are moral and spiritual beings submerged in unfathomable mystery from the very moment of our conception, and that therefore, even at our wisest, not only is it healthy for us to submit ourselves to the community that carries that ongoing reflection, but it is indeed our only hope.

But note—it takes a certain posture of soul to engage the wisdom of community rightly. "True discernment," Moses says, "is obtained *only when one is really humble.* The first evidence of this humility is when everything done or thought is submitted to the scrutiny of our elders. . . . Someone who lives not by his own decisions but by the example of the ancients will never be deceived."[9]

I recognize that the word *submit* has become cringeworthy in our day. There's no getting around it—it's a difficult word, not least because the folks that would *seem* to be worthy of our submission often prove themselves to be spiritually blind—or worse, corrupt. Countless are the stories of people whose faith was shipwrecked by spiritually blind, corrupt, oftentimes abusive leaders. The results are catastrophic. God forgive us.

But even here, the desert tradition is more than well aware of this peril, which is why—again—it is not simply a matter of cleaving to this or that *leader* (although it was crucial to have an "abba" or an "amma" who watched over your soul and who you sought to imitate; more on this later) but, more broadly, of cleaving *to the total communion of saints*. To illustrate, Moses tells a story of a young man who brought a lifelong struggle to an *apparent* "abba," only to leave full of despair that he could ever be holy. He would have left his monastic vows entirely had not *another* abba—one who was *genuinely* wise—intercepted him, offering him consolation and better counsel (and rebuking the first abba in the process!).[11]

The point is that *we need the church in its entirety*. One of the things I often hear people say nowadays is, "I need a mentor" or, "I am looking for someone to become my spiritual father/mother." I understand the need. But I think the impulse to cleave to a single individual at the expense of the multitude of relationships offered to us in the body of Christ is a mistake. It assumes that one person can lead us in the way of salvation. They cannot. But Christ—the total Christ, operating through the entirety of the community of faith, across time and geography and in the lives of all of those who surround us now—*can*.

Which is why I have often said that in my own life, a constellation of relationships have kept me sane and sound, guiding me to God. Here are just a few:

- my pastor
- my elders
- my colleagues (other pastors) on staff at my church
- my spiritual director
- fathers and mothers in the faith at my church
- brothers and sisters in the faith at my church
- fathers and mothers and brothers and sisters *beyond* my church

- my wife, my parents, my siblings
- my therapist
- mentors and coaches I've had in the past . . .

not to mention the witness of the saints preserved in their writings down through the centuries. I could go on and on. The point is that *Jesus is saving Andrew through his people!* Which is the only way he saves anyone—as by faith he unites us to his body, which is the church.

It's not easy. Our ingrained pride and selfishness make submitting to the voice of the Lord as it comes to us through his people challenging. Deeply challenging. But it always bears fruit. Recall the story of John the Dwarf submitting himself to an older monk who took a piece of dry wood, planted it in the ground, and told John to water it every day until it bore fruit. As the story goes:

> Now the water was so far away that he had to leave in the
> evening and return the following morning. At the end
> of three years the wood came to life and bore fruit. Then
> the old man took some of the fruit and carried it to the
> church saying to the brethren, "Take and eat the fruit of
> obedience."[12]

This story illustrates a central point of desert spirituality: that Christ, operating through the communion of saints, *knows things that we don't*—and that as we submit ourselves to him in robust relationship with the communion of saints, we discover, beyond our wildest expectations, that our lives have become fruitful.

CHAPTER 5

SAVED INTO COMMUNITY

The Priority of People

Then we will no longer be infants, tossed back and forth by the waves, and blown here and there by every wind of teaching and by the cunning and craftiness of people in their deceitful scheming. Instead, speaking the truth in love, we will grow to become in every respect the mature body of him who is the head, that is, Christ. From him the whole body, joined and held together by every supporting ligament, grows and builds itself up in love, as each part does its work.

EPHESIANS 4:14-16

The more I become identified with God, the more will I be identified with all the others who are identified with Him. His Love will live in all of us. His Spirit will be our One Life, the Life of all of us and Life of God. . . . The ultimate perfection of the contemplative life is not a heaven of separate individuals, each one viewing his own private intuition of God; it is a sea of Love which flows through the One Body of all the elect.

THOMAS MERTON

MAYBE IT'S JUST because I'm a pastor, but Sunday mornings really are one of my favorite times of the week. After rising early and spending a couple hours in quiet prayer and preparation, I clean myself up and put on my best clothes and head on over to the neighborhood school that serves as a sanctuary for our congregation. I always drive over with anticipation.

The anticipation is all about the relationships. I love seeing these people. I love seeing Jeff and Joel and Lacinda and their smiling faces when I pull into the parking lot—members of our life-safety team who make sure we're safe and secure as we worship on Sundays. Shaking hands with them and walking into the building together as we catch up on each other's weeks is a joy. It fills me with life.

I love seeing Victoria and Susan and Collin when I head into the lobby. We exchange hellos and hugs and chat a bit on how the morning's setup went. Collin's kids, Gabby and Palmer and Elan, are typically floating around the lobby, running this or that errand for their dad (who serves as our executive pastor—I think his kids might be unpaid interns for our church), and I relish the opportunity to greet these little brothers and sisters as well. "Good morning, Pastor Andrew!" Gabby will say, with clarity and strength and warmth. It always makes me snap to attention.

"Good morning, Gabby! Good to see you."

"Good to see you, too," she'll reply. Grace is being exchanged. Strength is rushing in.

I start making my way into the gymnasium, where the activity's been going on for several hours—setup and rehearsal and sound check and all of that. A nice little cadre of volunteers has assembled, from every stage and walk of life. Young guys like John and Tony and Marcus and Connor, who arrive at the crack of dawn on Sundays to start the load-in process. Kids like Davin (not quite ten years old), who helps with our AV-tech team and does a bang-up job. Busy moms like Kaitlyn and Traci and Megan and Jenna who, amid all the tasks of motherhood, somehow find the bandwidth to make our church happen. Seasoned saints like Barrack and Ruth and Joel and Dave and Robin, who have walked with God for decades, know the terrain of the Kingdom like the back of their hands, and are therefore well-equipped to lead ministries of prayer and intercession for us. And sweet grandmamas in the faith like Linda, a recent widow who has found loving community in our church and gives the love back by greeting people at the door (often, with her grandson Levi in tow) for both of our morning services. I rally the troops and lead a huddle of encouragement and prayer before we head out to serve. I'm always awed that I get to pastor this group.

And when the doors fling open—that's when the joy literally pours in. Seeing spiritual fathers and mothers like Jim and Jeannine and Mark and Rosemary walk through the door and greeting them makes my soul come alive. Walking the halls and giving high fives to my little bros, Braden, Michael, and Brice—our congregation's answer to the "sons of thunder" who once graced the ranks of Jesus' disciples (Mark 3:17)—puts strength in my heart. Fist-bumping my brothers Travis and Matt; bending down low to tell Matt and Ashley's daughter Bella that she looks beautiful in her dress; bear-hugging Michael and Lisa, newlyweds in their fifties who I married off a couple years ago; and then standing up on the platform and looking out on a sea of faces, many of whom I know, some of whom I don't, as I issue the call, *"Come, let us worship the Lord . . ."* The whole thing just moves me. And even though the morning is always strenuous, I go home with fresh vitality. The life of God has been exchanged among the saints once again.

THE PRIORITY OF PEOPLE

The Desert Fathers and Mothers provide a witness to the centrality of relationships for life in the Kingdom. You'll recall the words of Abba Anthony, who said that "our life and our death is with our neighbor. If we gain our brother, we have gained God, but if we scandalize our brother, we have sinned against Christ." Now, it would be easy to brush past Anthony's words too quickly. *Yes, yes,* we think. *Of course how we treat people matters. Next subject, please.*

Well, not so fast. For the Desert Fathers and Mothers, there *is no "next subject."* This is it. While these men and women understand the many perils to "life together," they are also aware that relationships are (to use Rowan Williams' fine phrase) "where God happens"— that relationships are where and how God makes himself savingly available to us. Which is *why* we see in the Desert Fathers and Mothers a kind of studied fanaticism about the importance of *people.* People are not secondary to life in the Kingdom. Learning to be rightly related to people *is* the Kingdom.

Consider this statement from Abba Agathon. Toward the end of his life, Agathon remarked that "I tried never to go to sleep while I kept a grievance against anyone. Nor did I let anyone go to sleep while he had a grievance against me."[1] Many of us strive to do the first piece of this. At the end of every day, as I've mentioned, I take a few minutes for examination, giving thanks to God for the gifts that the day brought my way, asking for mercy where I've failed, and *releasing* into God's hands those who have wronged me. As I've practiced this, I've discovered what the saints have known for centuries: that I tend to rest better, waking up with more gratitude and joy in my heart. If you've never done this, I encourage you to give it a try. God hasn't made us to carry the burden of bitterness.

But how many of us can say with Agathon that not only do we not go to sleep with grievances against others but—more than that—*we don't let others go to sleep who may have grievances against us*? You can almost imagine Agathon rapping on the cell door of one of his brothers late one night and saying, "While I was doing the Examen I remembered a comment I made that may have dishonored you. On the chance that was the case, I am here to plead your forgiveness. Please don't let the sun go down on your anger with me."

The idea of a breakdown in relationship going on more than several hours was unthinkable to Agathon. That radical posture, that conviction about the importance of relationships, is everywhere in the desert tradition. John Cassian reported a time when he and some companions visited one of the hermits in Egypt. The hermit received them gladly, breaking his rule of fasting in order to show hospitality. "Why do you break your rule?" Cassian asked the hermit. The man replied, "Fasting is always possible but I cannot keep you here forever. . . . God's law demands from us perfect love. I receive Christ when I receive you, so I must do all I can to show you love. When I have said goodbye to you, I can take up my rule of fasting again."[2]

How incredibly tender. For the hermit, God in Christ walked through the door when the visitors arrived. Like when Abraham received the three visitors at Mamre and realized later that he had received God (Genesis 18), the visit was a nearly unspeakable honor. Even more, showing hospitality and enjoying fellowship with guests was a fundamental moral and spiritual obligation for this hermit.

Relationships must be our priority, for it is in and by them that salvation breaks into the world. In one remarkable story from the desert, a priest from a heretical sect known as the Manichees was on his way to visit someone from the same sect when night fell upon him. Knowing it was dangerous to stay outside, he sought shelter with one of the Egyptian hermits, but he was afraid that he would be recognized as a heretic and turned away. As the story goes:

> The hermit opened the door and knew who he was; he welcomed him joyfully, made him pray with him, gave him supper and a bed. The Manichaean lay thinking in the night and wondering, "Why was he not hostile to me? He is a true servant of God." At daybreak, he got up, and fell at his feet, saying, "After this I will be orthodox, and I shall not leave you." So he stayed with him.[3]

The heretic was converted from false doctrine not by an angry harangue but *by the generous hospitality of a man of God.* Throughout the accounts of the Desert Fathers and Mothers, people took priority. But why? And why do we struggle to put that same kind of priority on relationships in our day?

THE ONLY SALVATION

The level of priority we give to people has everything to do with our soteriology—that is, our theology of salvation. For many (like me) who came to faith in the evangelical movement of the last hundred years, our understanding of salvation was almost *essentially* individualistic. "If you died tonight," we were asked at the end of a church service, crusade, or revival meeting, "do you know where you'd spend eternity?" The invitation at that point was to enter a "personal relationship with Jesus," securing our eternal destiny. Walk the aisle. Pray the sinner's prayer. Maybe get baptized. You're good to go. Salvation signed, sealed, and delivered.

But I would like to gently suggest that this way of talking about salvation is theologically misleading on at least two fronts. In the first place, nowhere in the New Testament is the call to salvation ever framed in those terms: *If you died . . . where would you spend . . . ?* Jesus didn't talk about salvation that way. His invitation was at once simpler, more immediate, and more robust: "Repent, for the kingdom of heaven is at hand" (Matthew 4:17, KJ21). For Jesus, repentance was about aligning your life with the righteous reign of God *now*. When he called folks to "repent," he wasn't asking them questions about where they would spend eternity. He was inviting them to enter God's cosmos-renewing work *now*—which was being made manifest in his own person, life, and teaching.

Which leads to the second misleading part of how we talk about salvation: that somewhere along the line the irreducibly corporate dimension of salvation, so evident throughout the New Testament, dropped out of view. We call people to enter a "personal relationship with Jesus," while Jesus called people to "follow me" and then invited them to join the new community that he was creating—a community that would carry life-restoring blessing to the world. For Jesus, salvation was inescapably corporate. God was restoring relationship not only between himself and human beings but also between *human beings and one another*.

And the early church understood it that way as well. Think

about the birth of the church described by Luke in Acts 2. The Spirit is poured out on the 120 disciples assembled in the upper room, and they spill into the streets, speaking in other tongues and prophesying. Standing up amid the shocked, gathered crowd, Peter preaches the first Christian sermon—on how the death and resurrection of Jesus is the fulfillment of every Old Testament hope and promise and how God had installed Jesus as both Lord of all and Messiah over the whole world. The group is "cut to the heart" and asks, "What can we do to be saved?"

Peter replies, "Repent and be baptized, every one of you, in the name of Jesus Christ for the forgiveness of your sins. And you will receive the gift of the Holy Spirit. The promise is for you and your children and for all who are far off—for all whom the Lord our God will call" (Acts 2:38-39). And they respond! Three thousand people are baptized.

But notice—Luke doesn't say that they are baptized and thereby enter a personal relationship with Jesus (although that is certainly true). He remarks that three thousand people were "added to *their* number" that day (Acts 2:41, emphasis mine). To be as clear as possible—for Luke (as for the rest of the New Testament writers), *the impact of God's saving work in Christ is the Spirit's creation of a new community of people, who together are being saved for the salvation of the world.* Listen to how Luke ends his account of that very first Pentecost Sunday:

> They devoted themselves to the apostles' teaching and to fellowship, to the breaking of bread and to prayer. Everyone was filled with awe at the many wonders and signs performed by the apostles. All the believers were together and had everything in common. They sold

property and possessions to give to anyone who had need. Every day they continued to meet together in the temple courts. They broke bread in their homes and ate together with glad and sincere hearts, praising God and enjoying the favor of all the people. And the Lord added to their number daily those who were being saved.

ACTS 2:42-47

The call to salvation is the call to join with this people who are together being made a kind of new humanity for the sake of the world. Through the common life of the church—where the Life of God courses through them as blood rushes through a body—the world is swept up into salvation. And that salvation simply *is* this new life of prayer and praise and thanksgiving and sharing life and meeting together and breaking bread and holding all things in common. If the immediate impact of the curse of sin in Genesis 3 and 4 is alienation and estrangement, then the immediate impact of the *undoing* of that curse is reconciliation and joyful relationship with God and others. From cover to cover, this is what the Bible is about.

Which lends some perspective to what Paul is doing in Ephesians—one of the most robust little treatises on the nature of salvation found in all the New Testament. After declaring that the church is "the fullness of him [Jesus Christ] who fills everything in every way" (Ephesians 1:23); that in the church the barrier between Jew and Gentile has been broken down (Ephesians 2:14); and that because of that fact the church is the place where "the manifold wisdom of God [is being] made known to the rulers and authorities in the heavenly realms" (Ephesians 3:10), Paul goes on to talk about just how that wisdom is implemented in the world:

through the building up of the body of Christ. He concludes one section of this teaching with this statement:

> Until we all reach unity in the faith and in the knowledge of the Son of God and become mature, attaining to the whole measure of the fullness of Christ.
> EPHESIANS 4:13

Now just think about that. Salvation, according to Paul, is the maturing of the entire community of faith *as* the body of Christ in the world, until finally, at the end of all things, we *together* arrive at the fullness of Christ.

The fourteenth-century Italian Doctor of the church Saint Catherine of Siena drove at this very thing when she compared the relationship between an individual and the community of faith to a vineyard:

> Keep in mind that each of you has your own vineyard. But every one is joined to your neighbors' vineyards without any dividing lines. They are so joined together, in fact, that you cannot do good or evil for yourself without doing the same for your neighbors.
>
> All of you together make up one common vineyard, the whole Christian assembly, and you are all united in the vineyard of the mystic body of holy Church from which you draw your life. In this vineyard is planted the vine, my only-begotten Son, into whom you must be engrafted. Unless you are engrafted into him you are rebels against holy Church, like members that are cut off from the body and rot.[4]

The conclusion is inescapable: The only salvation that God has or ever will offer us is in community. And not just *any* community but this very community known as the church: multiethnic; multigenerational; comprised of every race, class, and gender; cutting across every human-made divide; sweeping all kinds and sorts of people up into the Kingdom.

One of the finest theologians of the last century, the late Robert Jenson, has written as eloquently as any on the corporate nature of salvation. In one place, he remarked that a "body" is how persons are "available" to one another—my body simply *is* how I am present in the world to act and to make myself known—and as such, the "body of Christ" is, quite simply, how Christ is available to the world.[5] The community is where and how the Resurrected One is present amid the ebb and flow of history.

WE ARE THE CHURCH

One night some years ago, I came home from church and opened my computer to read a suddenly popular meme floating around social media: "I am the church." The meme, so far as I understood it, was intended as a kind of protest against the institutionalization of the church through paid religious professionals, versus the church as lived out by the everyday Christian.

I get the impulse. I really do. We desperately need to remember that the "church" is not merely a gathering orchestrated by clergy. It's also a sending and a scattering, a decentralized movement of God's people in the world.

But as a descriptive statement, "I am the church" is pure nonsense. The church by definition (the Greek *ekklésia* simply *means* "gathering") is a communion, a company, a body, a place where

God meets us in "others." I am not the church. And neither are you. But together, in Christ, by the power of the Spirit, *we are the church*.

Which means that I cannot be what I have been called to be in Christ apart from you. And you cannot be what you have been called to be apart from me. And no one can be what they have been called to be apart from all the others the Lord has called—for they all are how the total Christ (to steal a phrase from Augustine[6]) is present to enrich and bless and save our lives.

The practical tragedy of "I am the church" theology is that it philosophically underwrites the loneliness that is epidemic in our culture. Mother Teresa actually said that this was *the* poverty of the Western world: "The greatest disease in the West today is not TB [tuberculosis] or leprosy; it is being unwanted, unloved, and uncared for. We can cure physical diseases with medicine, but the only cure for loneliness, despair, and hopelessness is love. There are many in the world who are dying for a piece of bread but there are many more dying for a little love."[7]

God has designed the church to be the place where the disease of being unloved is healed. As love is given and received among the people of God, we are made whole. We grow up into our salvation. Thomas Merton more or less summarized the entire desert tradition on this point:

> The more I become identified with God, the more will I be identified with all the others who are identified with Him. His Love will live in all of us. His Spirit will be our One Life, the Life of all of us and Life of God. . . .
>
> The ultimate perfection of the contemplative life is not a heaven of separate individuals, each one viewing his

own private intuition of God; it is a sea of Love which flows through the One Body of all the elect.[8]

This call to community is beautiful and hard, for a number of reasons. We live in a very transient society where we are more mobile than ever, hopping from city to city and from church to church. The lack of rootedness in deep, long-term relationships spoils spiritual growth.[9]

On this the Desert Fathers and Mothers were in unanimous agreement. Amma Syncletica counseled, "If you find yourself in a monastery do not go to another place, for that will harm you a great deal. Just as the bird who abandons the eggs she was sitting on prevents them from hatching, so the monk or the nun grows cold and their faith dies, when they go from one place to another."[10] Transience was as much a problem then as it is now, and we're similarly going to need to learn the value of staying put in community— as far as it depends on us—if we expect to grow spiritually. As Abba Anthony said, "In whatever place you live, do not easily leave it."[11]

Which leads to the second difficulty. One of the reasons we *don't* stay put in community is that we've been hurt. When a significant breakdown in relationship occurs, it always seems easier to just move on. Trust me, I get it. I've spent my entire life in the church, and while the church has been the greatest blessing of my life (I've often said that not a single significant good thing has come to me except by way of the church), it has also been a significant source of wounding. In fact, it has been *the* most significant source of wounding. I might go so far as to say that the wounds have cut as deep as they have *in proportion to* the blessing that the church has been. The power for life, used wrongly, can be deadly.

Maybe we should be honest here. If we spend any significant

length of time among the people of God, we will get hurt. Jesus knows this, which is why smack in the middle of the prayer he taught his followers to pray, he said, "And forgive us our trespasses, as we forgive those who trespass against us." And then he closes his teaching on prayer by expanding on that line: "For if you forgive other people when they sin against you, your heavenly Father will also forgive you. But if you do not forgive others their sins, your Father will not forgive your sins" (Matthew 6:14-15).

Hurts will happen in community. Offenses will come. The only hope we have of being a community over the long haul is by continually opening ourselves up to the flow of God's forgiving grace—to us and through us to other people.

The New Testament vision of a mature community is only possible as we learn to forgive. When we do, the wounds we suffer at one another's hands are ultimately, like Christ's, healed—*as they are transfigured in resurrection life*. Which is precisely where Paul's teaching in Ephesians 4 leads: "Be kind and compassionate to one another, forgiving each other, just as in Christ God forgave you" (Ephesians 4:32). When we walk in forgiveness, resurrection life washes our wounds clean, lifting them up in healing grace. As one of the world's leading trauma researchers, Besser van der Kolk, has said, "Our capacity to destroy one another is matched by our capacity to heal one another. Restoring relationships and community is central to restoring well-being"[12]—which is, as it turns out, what the church has been saying for two thousand years.

But there's a third difficulty here, and it is a difficulty as basic as it gets: We are sinful, selfish people who just don't want to open our lives to others for fear of what will happen when we do. We'd rather nurse the delusion that we're fine, that we know everything we need to know (and that if we don't, we at least know how to find out), that we're gleefully independent and self-sufficient . . . than take the risk of entering deep community, where it will soon become apparent that we're *not* fine, that we *don't* know everything we need to know, and that we're not nearly as independent and self-sufficient as we thought.

THREE RELATIONSHIPS

Only when we humble ourselves enough to enter rich relationship with others can we discover how deeply and thoroughly God desires to save and bless us. But what do these relationships look like? Scripture and the witness of the Desert Fathers and Mothers commend to us three kinds of relationships, each of which enriches us and contributes to our sanctification. These relationships move in specific directions: "up," "across," and "down."

Up

One of the great gifts of the community of faith is that it teaches us to learn to relate "up" in relationship. For some of us—thanks to growing up with wise and trustworthy parents, or finding ourselves at some point under the tutelage of great teachers, coaches, or mentors—this kind of relationship may be familiar and easier to identify and access. But for many others, the thought of entering this kind of relationship—with someone further down the path; someone who knows more and sees further; someone who, through the benefit of age and wisdom, can see through our phony pretenses and shallow excuses; someone who can offer us correction or tell us no—well, for many people, that thought makes their heart race and their mouth dry. *Thanks, but no thanks.*

But underneath all that fear, I believe, is a longing. Longing for wisdom and counsel. Longing for direction. Longing for the blessing of a mother or a father. A longing for someone to identify what is good and right in us and cheer us on as we run toward the Kingdom. The community of faith gives us that. Think about young Timothy and the apostle Paul—the books of 1 and 2 Timothy simply *drip* with the affection and affirmation of a spiritual father for a young man in the faith. A little further back, think about John (the likely author of the fourth gospel), whom scholars believe was a teenager when he joined the ranks of Jesus' disciples. This is the disciple who often reclined at Jesus' chest—the affection of a younger brother for an older brother on full display.

Relationships like these, I believe, are a reflection of that most basic relationship in the universe—the relationship between the Father and the Son. John himself wrote that "no one has ever seen God, but the one and only Son, who is himself God and is in closest relationship with the Father, has made him known" (John 1:18). The Greek for "in closest relationship" actually denotes a physical posture ("against the chest of the Father" might be closer to the mark) and is the same linguistic construction that John uses to talk about how he leaned against the chest of Jesus. One relationship mirrored the other.

The desert tradition is a long practice in having relationships "up." The longing for an "abba" or an "amma" to give counsel and point the way was what drove people into the desert, and what they found (generally) were wise men and women who combined truthful speech with deep affection. Think of Paul's words: "Speaking the truth *in love*, we will grow to become in every respect the mature body of him who is the head, that is, Christ" (Ephesians 4:15, emphasis mine).

They did that. And the church provides ample opportunities for us to experience the same thing. If you'll open your eyes, you'll see that spiritual fathers and mothers (and spiritual big brothers and sisters) are everywhere. Chances are they're not advertising themselves *as* spiritual mothers and fathers. (In fact, in the desert tradition, one sure sign that a person *wasn't* spiritually trustworthy was that they actively sought out followers. Let the reader understand . . .) Generally, they're just living quiet, holy, decent, fruitful lives. They have a wholesomeness about them that makes you think they know something you don't. Seek them out. Ask if you can take them to breakfast or coffee sometime. Come with some questions ready. Give them space to tell their story. Ask for advice on this or that thing you're wrestling with.

After you've spent some time putting what they've told you into practice (and not until[13]), hit them up again. Give them a report on how it's all going, and repeat the process. Your life will be strengthened by it.

Across

One of the other great gifts the community of faith gives us is the chance to relate "across" in genuine relationships with peers in the faith. Folks who are in the same place (or thereabouts) in the journey of faith as you are. As such, they can offer (limited) counsel on what you're walking through but also—and maybe more importantly—camaraderie and sympathy, since they are experiencing many of the same things.

One of the very wonderful pictures that emerges from the desert is precisely that—groups of monks who together became little bands of brothers and sisters (under the tutelage of an abba or an amma) joyfully living and working together, learning and leaning into the life of holiness with each other, discovering Jesus along the way, as the two disciples did on the road to Emmaus (Luke 24). In this way, the desert experience becomes a reflection of what the Twelve experienced as they followed Jesus. We get glimpses of it here and there in the Gospels. The love. The togetherness. The iron-sharpening-iron conflicts. And all of it supervised by the wise and loving care of the Master, Jesus.

God intends for us to experience all of that through the church. I have been blessed and am blessed to this day with brothers and sisters—genuine peers—with whom I get to share life's joys and struggles and heartaches. Mandi and I are so grateful for people like this. Grateful for friends like Joe and Anj, Nathan and Shannon, Dave and Janie, Daniel and Lisa—people who have stood with us in the fiery furnace, who know us through and through, who love us dearly, who would jump on a plane at the drop of a hat to come and be with us if the *you-know-what* hit the fan. People like that are invaluable. They are the gift of God to us.

And they are also, generally, not hard to find. Join a small group at your church. Or volunteer somewhere. Or just strike up a conversation with someone after a service. One of the things I've learned is that the Spirit has a funny way of drawing like-minded and like-hearted brothers and sisters in the church together for their strengthening and edification. The Irish poet and philosopher John O'Donohue introduced the world to the phrase "anam ċara" in a book by the same name—a Gaelic expression meaning *soul friend*, that is, people you feel a natural affinity for, as if they were long-lost siblings.[14] Learn to recognize these folks when they come along—God is "refamilying" you by them!

Down

Finally, the church also provides opportunities for us to learn to relate in healthy ways "down," toward little brothers and sisters in the faith who *need* wisdom and counsel and blessing and, here and there, a helping hand.

I love this aspect of being part of the church. For me, as a dad, it starts with my kids—four disciples of Jesus who I am, as a fellow disciple, called to nurture and shepherd and protect. My kids give me the opportunity to enter the care that Christ Jesus showed to little ones so often in the Gospels, and as a follower of Jesus, my daily prayer is that my relationship with my kids would be governed by the model he gave.

Beyond that, the many kids and younger believers in my congregation give me a chance to *be* a spiritual father/big brother for others, and I relish those opportunities. I don't take them lightly. When I bend down to look Gabby and Palmer and Elan in the eye on Sunday as I greet them, in my heart I know I'm showing something of the face of Christ to them. And when younger believers seek me out to ask questions about faith and life, I eagerly say yes, knowing that I'm being given an opportunity to give away what I've been given by others—so that, through the interaction, the gift of God goes on and on. It's a privilege to be part of the means by which Jesus Christ is raising up the young ones in our midst.

A word of caution here. As I mentioned earlier, for the Desert Fathers and Mothers, one of the sure marks that a person is *not* fit to be a spiritual father or mother is (perhaps paradoxically) an overeagerness to *be* a spiritual father or mother. Self-designated spiritual fathers and mothers are folks to be avoided. Someone came to Abba Poemen once and said, "Some brothers live with me; do you want me to be in charge of them?" Poemen replied, "No, just work first and foremost, and if they want to live like you, they will see to it themselves." The man was frustrated and said to Poemen, "But it is they themselves, Father, who want me to be in charge of them." Poemen replied, "No, be their example, not their legislator."[15]

I think that's excellent advice. Too many folks nowadays are altogether too eager to create a following for themselves, to take charge over others. With the breakdown of the family accelerating at an alarming rate and the hunger for coaching and mentoring rising each day, it is easier than ever to draw a crowd, to pull people into your little self-appointed "circle of influence," and then to position yourself publicly as a kind of spiritual guru. I hear people say sometimes, "I'm trying to reproduce myself in the next generation," and I think, *Please, don't. One of you is enough, thanks.*

Instead of that, I wonder if we can't just live the right way in community, in a way that serves as an example to others, modeling the Christ who refused to collect for himself power and influence but instead routinely gave it away. He loved even his own life not so much as to shrink back from death—leaving a pattern for us to follow.

CHAPTER 6

RESTORED THROUGH COMMUNITY

Paul repeatedly identifies Christ and the church-community . . .
Where the body of Christ is, there Christ truly is. . . .
The church is the presence of Christ in the
same way that Christ is the presence of God.
DIETRICH BONHOEFFER

The Church is a mystery; that is to say she is also a sacrament. . . .
In this world she is the sacrament of Christ, as Christ himself,
in his humanity, is for us the sacrament of God.
HENRI DE LUBAC

Abba Agathon said, "If I could meet a leper, give him my body and
take his, I should be very happy." That indeed is perfect charity.
AS TOLD IN *THE SAYINGS OF THE DESERT FATHERS*

W E TOOK COMMUNION about once a quarter in the church of my childhood. Maybe less. As such, the meaning of the sacrament tended to go over my head when I was a kid.

On one occasion, when I was very young, after the tray of grape juice went by, the small wicker basket of oyster crackers wound up in my hands. I took a big handful, for which my mom quickly, and graciously, corrected me—*one cracker will do; hold on to it and to your tiny cup of juice until the preacher tells us what to do.*

He did, and the service plodded along for several more minutes before my mom looked down to see tears flowing down my cheeks. Thinking that her oldest son was simply overcome with the awesome power of the blessed sacrament, she leaned over and asked, "Andrew, what is the matter?" Instantly, I replied, through sobs, "I'm still *hungry* . . ."

So much for "whoever comes to me will never go hungry" (John 6:35), right?

Thankfully, my sense of the meaning of the sacrament of Communion has grown as I've grown in my faith. Though I've served exclusively in non-denominational churches since leaving seminary back in 2006, each of those churches has followed the pattern of the historical church, making the Table the centerpiece and culmination of worship. I could probably count on two hands the number of Sundays I've missed the Eucharist during those years. It has formed, and is forming, me in deep ways.

At the simplest level, Communion reminds me that the most important thing about me, you, or anyone else is not what we can do for God but what God can do and does for us in Jesus Christ. Paul said that "he who began a good work in you will carry it on to completion until the day of Christ Jesus" (Philippians 1:6) and elsewhere that "from him and through him and for him are all things" (Romans 11:36). Without the Table to govern and guide it, worship and preaching can devolve into pseudo-Coldplay concerts and loosely-based-on-Scripture TED talks masquerading as the gospel—human-centered strategies for transcendence and self-improvement. But week after week at the Table, I am reminded that, from the first to the last, the gospel is about God's mercy to sinners, and God's mercy—not our efforts—is what defines our lives.

Second, Communion reminds me that matter, well, *matters*. That the gospel is not a set of ideas that we think upon savingly but, rather, is indeed the announcement that—because of Christ's resurrection from the dead and the pouring out of the Spirit at Pentecost—the transformation of created reality is at hand. Like the burning bush on Mount Horeb (Exodus 3), the bread and wine of Communion, without ceasing to be bread and wine, are lifted up and made vehicles for the divine presence to come and renew our lives. As Paul says, "Is not the cup of thanksgiving for which we give thanks a participation in the blood of Christ? And is not the bread that we break a participation in the body of Christ?" (1 Corinthians 10:16). The sign and the Signified, the symbol and the Symbolized coinhere at the Table. When I come to Communion every week, with the eyes of faith I am seeing bread and wine transfigured by the divine presence so that my life and the lives of my fellow worshipers may also be transfigured by the divine presence—the same presence that will one day flood our cosmos, renewing all things. "Behold," the Lord says, "I make all things new" (Revelation 21:5).

Communion reminds me: That is where we are headed. One day, war, racism, and genocide; plague, pestilence, and famine; broken bodies, broken minds, and broken hearts—all of it will be a thing of the past. The curse of sin will finally be overcome, and all creation will flourish—and us along with it. Each week when we gather at the Table, my heart throbs with longing for the day when the Voice from heaven resounds with a shout, announcing the full and final arrival of the new creation.

But there is more. And I think it speaks not only to the deep identity of who we are called to be as God's people, but it also solves a riddle at the heart of the witness of the Desert Fathers and Mothers.

A RIDDLE

Now it is time to draw fully out into the open something I've alluded to throughout this book—a posture, an orientation, the deep under-current of the spirituality of the Desert Fathers and Mothers.

Consider this story about Abba Poemen:

> Some old men came to see Abba Poemen and said to him, "When we see brothers who are dozing at the synaxis, shall we rouse them so that they will be watchful?" He said to them, "For my part, when I see a brother who is dozing, I put his head on my knees and let him rest."[1]

Now, as always, it would be easy to brush past this little story as an example of a simple act of compassion offered by an older monk to a younger. *Yes, yes—let's not be too hard on one another*, we might think. And we wouldn't be wrong if that were the conclusion we drew. But we also wouldn't be *right enough*. There's more going on here.

The story says that the old men were asking him about the "synaxis." *Synaxis* is a Greek word that referred to the liturgical gathering of the monks, usually on the weekends. It was a service of worship and prayer. And at the heart of it was—you guessed it—the celebration of the Lord's Table.

So the old men are frustrated because some of the younger monks are falling asleep during this highest and holiest ritual. They want confirmation from Poemen that this laxity in worship demands a severe response. But instead, Poemen replies with an answer so tender, so humane—so wildly reminiscent, frankly, of Jesus.

One of the things that always strikes me when I read the Gospels is how tender and humane Jesus is. People and their real needs were always a central concern of his. Consider this moment from the Gospel of Mark:

> One Sabbath Jesus was going through the grainfields, and as his disciples walked along, they began to pick some heads of grain. The Pharisees said to him, "Look, why are they doing what is unlawful on the Sabbath?"
>
> He answered, "Have you never read what David did when he and his companions were hungry and in need? In the days of Abiathar the high priest, he entered the house of God and ate the consecrated bread, which is lawful only for priests to eat. And he also gave some to his companions."
>
> Then he said to them, "The Sabbath was made for man, not man for the Sabbath. So the Son of Man is Lord even of the Sabbath."
>
> MARK 2:23-28

The disciples are breaking the Sabbath. This is a big no-no. For the Jewish people, Sabbath was more than just a day of rest.

It was a weekly sign of their covenant with the God who delivered them from the furnace of Egypt, leading them into a land flowing with milk and honey, where they could live and move and have their being in peace and prosperity (Deuteronomy 5:12-15; Acts 17:28). So, to dishonor or disregard the Sabbath was a great offense. It was to treat the Lord's deliverance and promise with contempt. The Pharisees were not wrongly fanatical about the Sabbath. The rules were in place to protect something precious and important.

And Jesus aims to protect that as well—which makes what he says so astounding. He sees beyond the surface application of the Sabbath rules to the deep will of God for humanity. "The Sabbath was made for man," he says, "not man for the Sabbath." The disciples are hungry. Sabbath is God's sign in the midst of history that he would have their bellies—and every belly—full. Yes, there are rules, says Jesus. And yes, the rules matter. But the point of the rules is the flourishing of people, and if we can't see the connection between the two, we'll wildly misinterpret and misapply the rules. This is the deep humanness of our Savior.

Another story from the Gospel of Matthew that gets at this same point:

> Going on from that place, he went into their synagogue, and a man with a shriveled hand was there. Looking for a reason to bring charges against Jesus, they asked him, "Is it lawful to heal on the Sabbath?"
>
> He said to them, "If any of you has a sheep and it falls into a pit on the Sabbath, will you not take hold of it and lift it out? How much more valuable is a person than a sheep! Therefore it is lawful to do good on the Sabbath."

Then he said to the man, "Stretch out your hand." So he stretched it out and it was completely restored, just as sound as the other.

MATTHEW 12:9-13

Once again, this behavior frustrated the Pharisees. Matthew remarks right after this that they "went out and plotted how they might kill Jesus" (Matthew 12:14), and Jesus felt the need to steal away from that place as a result. But the crowds follow (as they always do), and Jesus heals everyone who is ill (Matthew 12:15), warning them not to tell about him (Matthew 12:16). And Matthew says that this fulfills the word of the prophet Isaiah:

Here is my servant whom I have chosen,
    the one I love, in whom I delight;
I will put my Spirit on him,
    and he will proclaim justice to the nations.
He will not quarrel or cry out;
    no one will hear his voice in the streets.
A bruised reed he will not break,
    and a smoldering wick he will not snuff out,
till he has brought justice through to victory.
    In his name the nations will put their hope.

MATTHEW 12:18-21[2]

A bruised reed he won't break, a smoldering wick he won't snuff out—until justice comes, the final victory of God over all that mars and defaces human life. And therefore, says Matthew (quoting Isaiah), in his name the nations will put their hope. For he is the Great Physician, the Healer, the Restorer, the one who finally makes right all that the enemy has made wrong in God's good world. And none of his plans will fail.

It is this very reality—the reality of *this Christ*, the Restorer, with us and for us forever—that Poemen is living from in his tenderness toward the younger brothers. *The same Christ that defended the hungry disciples and healed on the Sabbath was present in Poemen's words and actions.* Poemen was not just "being nice." He was living Christ. And letting Christ live in him. And that, I believe, is the heart of desert spirituality—the realization of the Christ-life in our midst.

When you get this, the deep motive behind some of the most beautiful and prophetic acts of the Desert Fathers and Mothers comes into focus. One of my favorite stories from the desert comes from Abba Bessarion: "A brother who had sinned was turned out of the church by the priest; Abba Bessarion got up and went with him, saying, 'I, too, am a sinner.'"[3]

Think about that. Bessarion made the brother's disgrace his own. Why would he do that? Even better—*who* does that remind you of?

Bessarion was living Christ with and for the brother. As Christ did for us—descending into human flesh and finally death on a cross in order to find us and bring us home—so Bessarion did for the one who was publicly disgraced. And though we don't know the end of the story, we can reasonably conclude—based on other stories like it—that Bessarion's actions led to the restoration of the brother and, so, the fuller unveiling of the reality of Christ in the world.

A similar story emerges from the life of Abba Anthony. A brother from a neighboring monastery was dealing with temptation. Rather than restoring the brother gently, his "abba" cast him out. The brother wandered to where Anthony was, and when Anthony learned his story, he sent him back to the monastery. The brothers there promptly expelled him again. When he wound up once more with Anthony, Anthony sent him back with this message:

> A boat was shipwrecked at sea and lost its cargo; with
> great difficulty it reached the shore; but you want to
> throw into the sea that which has found a safe harbor on
> the shore.

The story concludes: "When the brothers understood that it was Abba Anthony who had sent them this monk, they received him at once."[4] And there again: Through the actions of Anthony, the Jesus of the Gospels was making manifest his glory.

The great abbas and ammas of the desert repudiated the culture of throwing people away, a culture wholly opposed to the goal of Christ's Passion: to heal humanity, reconciling men and women to God. This was the light that guided how they related to one another—always, only, and ever, *savingly*. A story is told about Abba Achilles in which three men came to him with individual requests. One of the men had a bad reputation. The first two, Abba Achilles denied. The last, who had the bad reputation, Achilles obliged.

The first two were confused. Why oblige the man with the bad reputation and not them, they asked? Achilles' response is so telling:

> I told you I would not make one, and you were not
> disappointed, since you thought that I had no time. But

if I had not made one for him, he would have said, "The old man has heard about my sin, and that is why he does not want to make me anything," and so our relationship would have broken down. But now I have cheered his soul, so that he will not be overcome with grief.[5]

Achilles discerned the man's need and acted as Christ did—with surgical precision and utterly clear-minded spiritual insight—to lay the groundwork for restoration. And in this way, he embodied the infinite concern of God for the man with the bad reputation, knowing, as Paul says, that it is the kindness of God that leads sinners like us to repentance (Romans 2:4).

In the world of counseling psychology, Carl Rogers developed a groundbreaking insight: Only when the therapist showed unconditional positive regard for patients could those patients find healing. The Desert Fathers and Mothers knew this long before he did—and knew it in a deeper way:

> It was said of Abba Isidore, priest of Scetis, that when anyone had a brother who was sick, or careless or irritable, and wanted to send him away, he said, "Bring him here to me." Then he took charge of him and by his long-suffering he cured him.[6]

Willing to endure the weaknesses of others in a spirit of unconditional positive regard, until they found moral and spiritual rectitude—how like Jesus that is. No, we could say it better: How *Jesus* that is—for if what the Scripture teaches about our union with Jesus Christ is true, then it was none other than Jesus himself acting in Isidore to restore the weak brothers.

One particularly poignant example of the living of the Christ-life comes from Abba Agathon, who once said that "if I could meet a leper, give him my body and take his, I should be very happy."[7] Who says things like this? Only one who knows the God who in Christ bore our leprous bodies in his own body to make us whole again—and who calls us, as members of his body, to go and do likewise. Agathon's Christ-shaped, Christ-driven compassion was legendary, and it extended not just to brothers but to all whom he encountered:

> It was also said of him that, coming to the town one day to sell his wares, he encountered a sick traveler lying in the public place without anyone to look after him. The old man rented a cell and lived with him there, working with his hands to pay the rent and spending the rest of his money on the sick man's needs. He stayed there four months till the sick man was restored to health. Then he returned in peace to his cell.[8]

This episode could just as easily be read as a parable of how God has come to be with us in Jesus. For *Jesus* is the one who comes to our town, who encounters us sick in the public square without anyone to look after us, who remains among us as he works with his hands and spends all his money on our needs until we are restored to health. But Jesus refuses to leave us behind, instead carrying us with him to the heart of his Father in heaven, in which there is room enough for all of us (John 14:2).

THE BODY OF GOD

Back to where we started: the Table of the Lord.

The reason that the church has traditionally made Communion the centerpiece of her worship is not just that it is telling her something important about God. Communion is telling her something important about herself—indeed, the *most important things* she could ever know about God and herself.

I mentioned earlier two things that Communion reminds me of each week: first, that God and his work are the most important thing about you and me; and second, matter *matters*, and the transformation of all reality is where we are headed.

But there is a third thing.

Communion reminds me that the deep reality of the church is none other than the incarnate, crucified, risen, and returning Christ. Too often, we treat the church like a religiously themed social club or a weekly "Jesus pep rally," where we largely relate to Jesus and one another in an "external" and incidental way. Me "here" and you "over there" and Jesus "up there"—wherever *there* is.

But that is not the perspective of the New Testament. When we come, for instance, to Paul's letter to the Corinthians, we overhear him referring to the bread and wine of Communion as the "body and blood of the Lord" (1 Corinthians 10:16; 11:23-29)—without any qualification or hesitation. But then—note carefully—we *also* overhear him telling the Corinthians that "we were all baptized by one Spirit so as to form one body" (1 Corinthians 12:13), saying of the Corinthians themselves just a few verses later that "You *are* the body of Christ" (1 Corinthians 12:27, emphasis mine). Fascinating, isn't it? *Both* the bread and the cup *and* the gathered communion of saints are, to Paul's mind, the very body of Jesus of Nazareth.

Which means (among much else) that when we come to the Table, we are seeing *not only* Christ Jesus given to us in bread and cup, broken and poured out for the life of the world . . . we are *also*, and to the same extent, *seeing ourselves taken into Christ Jesus, broken and poured out for the life of the world.*[9] Both bread and cup and the gathered communion are, by the grace of God, a "re-presentation" of Christ to the world.

Saint Augustine drew attention to this very thing in a homily on the sacrament of Holy Communion:

> Believe what you see, see what you believe and become what you are: the Body of Christ. . . . If you, therefore, are Christ's body and members, it is your own mystery that is placed on the Lord's table! It is your own mystery that you are receiving! You are saying "Amen" to what you are.[10]

"Become what you are." That line represents perhaps the most profound thing I am reminded of each week at the Table. That what is taking shape in history, in the community I pastor, and in communities of faith all over the world is nothing less than what Dietrich Bonhoeffer wrote of: "Where the body of Christ is, there Christ truly is," and "*The church is the presence of Christ in the same way that Christ is the presence of God.*"[11]

The church, we may therefore say in full consistency with the witness of the New Testament, *is the body of the Christ who is the body of God in the world.* It is the ongoing *em*bodiment of the mystery of God-with-us in Christ.

As Robert Jenson says so well, "The church is not a plurality of persons held together by common commitment," but rather "we receive one another with Christ and Christ with one another" at the Table; "we at once receive Christ and the church in which we receive him."[12] The intimate union between body and head, the church and her Lord, and each member one with another is declared and strengthened at the Table: The church is "re-membered" as she remembers that what binds her together, what makes her what she is, and what shapes her being and destiny is not the weakness of mutual human affection but Jesus Christ himself—God's indestructible love and life made flesh, made *our* flesh. In Christ Jesus, we are made members of the body of God—for one another, with one another, and all together for the life of the world.

Which changes the way we look at what it means to be in the community known as the church. If what the Table bears witness to is true, then the very last thing we can be is casual or cavalier about our connection to each other, or thoughtless about how we relate to each other and to the world around us. I have been arguing that for the Desert Fathers and Mothers, relation-ships were primary. And now we see the full magnitude of why: because in and through the church, God in Christ by the power of the Spirit is "embodying" himself in the world. And there-fore, if we are being true to the central claims of our faith, we are fanatical about our one-another-ness. As Paul writes, "Make every effort to keep the unity of the Spirit through the bond of peace" (Ephesians 4:3). Not *create* the unity. But *keep* it. Because our unity is a gift—the gift of Jesus Christ himself—meant to be cherished and stewarded wisely.

During the tumultuous cultural and political season of 2020, one of the things that disturbed me was how many people left our church and many churches around the country either because of how those churches handled the COVID-19 pandemic (or how they failed to handle it) or because of what those churches said (or didn't say) about race riots or because of where those churches fell (or didn't fall) on the political spectrum. Some went to churches that they felt more fully aligned with their convictions about those matters. Many more stopped attending church altogether.

The issues are complex; I get it. And I know that many who left their churches did so out of a sense of faithfulness to Jesus, grieved by the unhealth they perceived. Sometimes moving on is not just warranted but demanded by the call of conscience.

Still, I wonder. Was *all* of the church movement demanded by a call of conscience? How much does it reveal the extent to which we are still slaves to those things that are not gods—to politics, race, power, and the like? And even more—how much does it reveal our unwillingness to enter the kind of healthy conflict and hospitality to different perspectives and convictions that is characteristic of the Kingdom?

If our demand is for Jesus, not Jesus *plus* whatever our pet issue is, I think, frankly, that we will fight harder for unity than most of us are willing to. Our failure to fight for it reveals that we have not yet fully surrendered ourselves to the truth of our baptism. As it stands, the gods of this age are still inflicting wounds upon the body of Christ.

THROUGH AND IN JESUS CHRIST

Imagine if we believed Dietrich Bonhoeffer's words that "Christianity means community through Jesus Christ and in Jesus Christ" and "no Christian community is more or less than this."[13] How would it change the way that we approached our life with one another as witnesses to the world of the Life of God who is Jesus Christ?

I think if we grasped this, we would become a people of

uncommon humility who refuse to live judgmentally toward one another. Just before his admonition to keep the unity of the Spirit, Paul wrote, "Be completely humble and gentle; be patient, bearing with one another in love" (Ephesians 4:2). Humility is the indispensable foundation for the practice of unity. And the reason that we can live this way is because, in the cross and resurrection of Christ, we are continually grasping the fact that we are no better than anyone else.

"All have sinned and fall short of the glory of God," said Paul, "and all are justified freely by his grace through the redemption that came by Christ Jesus" (Romans 3:23-24). And so, Paul asked, "Where, then, is boasting?"—and answered, "It is excluded" (Romans 3:27). The pride that severs us from one another is destroyed at the cross.

And as a result? We live humbly, gently, and nonjudgmentally toward one another—that is to say, we live in ways that make room for God's healing to break in. A story of Abba Moses captures this so well:

> A brother at Scetis committed a fault. A council was
> called to which Abba Moses was invited, but he refused
> to go to it. Then the priest sent someone to say to him,
> "Come, for everyone is waiting for you." So he got up
> and went. He took a leaking jug, filled it with water and
> carried it with him. The others came out to meet him
> and said to him, "What is this, Father?" The old man
> said to them, "My sins run out behind me, and I do not
> see them, and today I am coming to judge the errors of
> another." When they heard that they said no more to the
> brother but forgave him.[14]

One of the ways we try to control other people's behavior is through our judgments. But this strategy fails from the start. Dallas Willard remarked, "It is extremely rare that anyone who is condemned will respond by changing in the desired way."[15] Much better, he thought, is to "abandon the deeply rooted human practice of condemning and blaming" so that "the power of God's kingdom will be more freely available to bless and guide those around us into his ways."[16]

But—take note—we can only really *become* such people to the extent that we learn, as Jesus taught, to take the plank out of our own eyes (Matthew 7:1-6). Growth in grace seems to be a growth not only in righteousness but also (and perhaps it is the same thing) *growth in our awareness of our faults.* Note that Moses is called "the old man" in this story. The older he got, the more he matured, the more clearly he grasped his own sinfulness—which in turn made him more humble, more merciful, and more of a healer.

Bonhoeffer says that as we exist for one another in and through Christ Jesus, we "meet one another as bringers of the message of salvation."[17] Humility and nonjudgment are a big part of that vocation, so that we—as Bonhoeffer goes on to say—no longer know each other through our own egos but only through the saving work of Christ. We need more of that in the church.

I think believing this would also make us a people of *uncommon commitment* to one another. Believing that Christ Jesus is not just the *basis* for our connection but is *himself* the connection inevitably strengthens our sense of our commitment to one another. No longer is our association based on personal preference or mere human affection—and certainly no longer on perfect alignment of theological or political beliefs or a common vision for how society should work—but on (and in) the one who died and was raised to life, that all things should finally be reconciled. As Bonhoeffer remarked, "We have one another only through Christ, but through Christ we do have one another, wholly, and for eternity."[18]

And so we stand for and with each other, even to death. Abba John the Dwarf said that the foundation of our spiritual life "is our neighbor, whom we must win. . . . All the commandments of Christ depend on this one."[19] To "win" our neighbor means that we are constantly cultivating and fighting for the Christ-depth of our relationship with one another—that it and it alone would win the day between us.

What that means in part is, short of condoning sin or heresy, we'll do whatever it takes to maintain our connection to one another. A humorous story about Abba Paul the Barber illustrates the point. While living with his brother Abba Timothy, Paul and Timothy fought constantly. Exasperated, Paul asked, "How long shall we go on like this?" Timothy suggested, "You take my side of the argument and in my turn I will take your side when you oppose me." So they did. As the story goes, "they spent the rest of their days in this practice"—no doubt in *peace* as well.[20]

Why would they do that? Because they knew that their connection to one another in Christ was more fundamental than any dispute they could have. So they become men of uncommon commitment. Imagine if Christians of rival political parties did that. What would that say to the world about what is possible?

Finally, I think living with this perspective—the formation of community in and through Christ—would make us a people of *uncommon love*: love for each other that spills out into how we behave toward the world around us, and through which the world is won to the glory and goodness of God. What becomes clear the more you read the Desert Fathers and Mothers is that the church at its best is a kind of "school of love"—a place where we learn new habits of relating to each other, habits that we in turn embody in our witness to the world.

Consider this story: "It was said of Abba John the Persian that when some evildoers came to him, he took a basin and wanted to wash their feet. But they were filled with confusion, and began to do penance."[21] Won to the Kingdom not through angry harangues or air-tight apologetics or urgent appeals for repentance but because John washed their feet. How about that?

Jesus had said at the Last Supper that as the disciples learned to wash one another's feet, so the world would know they belonged to him (John 13:35). And suppose they, in turn—like Jesus—turned that same love, that same practice, *outward* to the world?

That, it seems to me, is what it means to be witnesses.

PART THREE

INTO THE DESERT
FOR THE WORLD

A life rooted in and ordered to God in Christ
brings blessing to the world:
Our patterns of speech change
our work is sanctified
our lives become gifts given for the life of the world—
living miracles that bear witness to the Kingdom.

CHAPTER 7

SAVING SPEECH

Death and life are in the power of the tongue:
and they that love it shall eat the fruit thereof.
PROVERBS 18:21, KJV

Teach your mouth to say what is in your heart.
ABBA POEMEN

Abba Theodore of Pherme asked Abba Pambo, "Give me a word."
With much difficulty he said to him, "Theodore, go and have pity
on all, for through pity, one finds freedom of speech before God."
AS TOLD IN *THE SAYINGS OF THE DESERT FATHERS*

DEATH AND LIFE ARE IN THE TONGUE, Proverbs eighteen twenty-one . . ." I probably heard my mom quote that verse a thousand times in my childhood, as often as not accompanied by the second half: *"and those who love it will eat its fruit."* The writer of Proverbs is making one of those strobe-light observations, the kind that flash onto an area of our experience, lighting up *both* what is right *and* what is horribly wrong with us. The words of our mouths, the verse tells us, are powerful, capable of dealing life and death in equal measure. Whichever we are in love with—death or life—we will invariably use our tongues to advance. And we will reap in proportion to our sowing. Our lives, in large measure, are a product of what we have put into motion by what we have *said*— or what others have said to or about us. Words matter.

I grew up in a church community that knew the power of words and was determined to use them well—to bless, to build up, and to heal. Sometimes their words were just ordinary words of affirmation or encouragement. Other times they were more what we might call "prophetic" in nature—I can think of dozens of times someone or another would approach me with "Young man, I sense the Lord saying over you . . ." and then would speak words that formed holy identity, holy desire, and a sense of destiny in me. They sowed seeds of life in me—seeds that decades later are bearing fruit.

By the same token, when I think of the great griefs of my life (surely it is the same for you), many, if not all, of them are connected in some way with death-dealing words. I have had vicious cruelties spoken over me—some of which have taken decades to deconstruct. Our lives, like the lunar landscape, are pockmarked with the memory of reckless words.

Sadly, I have also spoken reckless words over others. When I was in tenth grade, I found myself very frustrated with one of my younger friends, a ninth grader I'll call Ben. He was a beautiful soul—vibrant, friendly, and funny. He could also be a touch awkward (but really, who isn't in ninth grade?) and often did outlandish things to try to win people's attention. While I loved Ben, I also was desperately eager to work my way into the good graces of a group of upperclassmen. When Ben one day launched into a fit of characteristic outlandishness, I—embarrassed by my association—lit into him, hoping to distance myself from my friend and also secure my belonging in the group of older students. As to the latter, it gained me nothing. As to the former, the verbal assault hurt Ben deeply and left me alienated from his family for some time. The wounds took years to heal. An early lesson. *Death and life . . .*

The writer of Proverbs elsewhere says, "The words of the reckless pierce like swords"—and how true it is—and then immediately adds, "but the tongue of the wise brings healing" (Proverbs 12:18). If our lives are going to go right, if our tongue is going to bring healing to the world, then our speech needs saving.

And here again—the Desert Fathers and Mothers can help.

FLEE, BE SILENT, PRAY ALWAYS

The Desert Fathers and Mothers were diligent about living the prayer of the psalmist: "Set a guard over my mouth, LORD; keep watch over the door of my lips" (Psalm 141:3). Indeed, they saw it as one of the most important tasks of the spiritual life. The wisdom of James was deeply embedded in their hearts: "Those who consider themselves religious and yet do not keep a tight rein on their tongues deceive themselves, and their religion is worthless" (James 1:26).

The spirituality of Abba Arsenius (or Arsenius the Great, as he was known to some), one of the greatest of the Desert Fathers, was marked by such a "tight rein." We have read before the story of his withdrawal from Roman imperial life, and we see the reflection of his philosophy of speech in the first two of his sayings:

> While still living in the palace, Abba Arsenius prayed to God in these words, "Lord, lead me in the way of salvation." And a voice came saying to him, "Arsenius, flee from men and you will be saved."

And then,

> Having withdrawn to the solitary life, he made the same prayer again and he heard a voice saying to him, "Arsenius, flee, be silent, pray always, for these are the sources of sinlessness."[1]

The juxtaposition of the sayings is noteworthy. Whatever discomfort Arsenius may have felt at the vanity of his former life, simply running away from it was not, nor could ever be, enough. A more radical flight was required—not just from people but from the whole network of malice, manipulation, and lies that comes from having a loose tongue. "Flee" is followed hard on the heels by the disciplines of silence and prayer. Silence tells the tongue where to halt. Prayer reorients it Godward.

For the fathers and mothers of the desert, the transformation of human speech begins there. Right there. They teach us that if our *lives* are going to go right, there must be a retraining of the *lips* in righteousness. Rowan Williams notes that "silence somehow reaches to the root of our human problem."[2] Lips, heart, and life are all interconnected. We're not talking about a few minor adjustments, either—a vocabulary nip here or lexical tuck there—but a complete overhaul. Our speech must be rebuilt from the ground up. Radical problems require radical solutions.

Professional athletes understand this. A top-ranked quarterback prospect will come out of college and into the pros thinking he's *all that*, only to meet a coach who knows better: The entire throwing motion will have to be overhauled if he's going to thrive at that next level of play. A professional golfer or NBA player will have a slump season and think a little recalibration will solve the problem, only to meet a swing consultant or a shot doctor who knows better: It's time to get back to the basics. The swing, the shot, must be rebuilt.

Sometimes the way forward is backward. Sometimes you have to break a thing down to its most elemental before you can transform it into something better. So said the writer of Ecclesiastes: "a time to kill and a time to heal, a time to tear down and a time to build" (Ecclesiastes 3:3). We don't like to think that way. We'd prefer that everything were progress, the unmitigated realization of our potential. Everything "healing" and "building."

But a great many things in life are simply not like that. And the spiritual life is *least of all* like that. Spirituality is not "progress." Salvation is not self-improvement. If our speech is going to rise to the level of the Kingdom of God, we'll have to pass through a kind of vocal purgatory first. Our verbal way of being must die before it can be brought to life. The writer of Ecclesiastes continues: "A time to be silent . . ." Silence first. Then, and then only, "*a time to speak*" (Ecclesiastes 3:7, emphasis mine).

The mortification of the tongue is a critical issue in the spirituality of the desert. Abba Agathon related that "no passion is worse than an uncontrolled tongue, because it is the mother of all the passions."[3] A person who gives free rein to whatever silly thought comes to their heads will soon find both their soul and the world around them engulfed in flames. You've probably noticed it. It starts when you're young. You make bawdy jokes or spread a little gossip to work your way into the in-group. Before long, the in-group is inflamed with your bawdiness, your gossip; and not only that, but *bawdy and contemptuous feelings* start growing up in your soul.

It's weird how that happens, isn't it? You didn't really mean what you said. It was just a little horsing around. But now, suddenly, those words have become a part of your outlook and attitude. Richard Foster observes, "The tongue is a thermometer; it gives our spiritual temperature." But, he continues, "it is also a thermostat; it regulates our spiritual temperature."[4] Let the reader understand.

When you're older, the subject matter tends to change, but the spiritual dynamic at work is the same. You slander someone you're trying to get an edge on at work; you write a "slam dunk" social-media post denouncing your political enemies; you make a racial joke to your colleagues. Sin rushes out of your mouth and meets sin in the public square. The people who listen to you, if they're not spiritually discerning, are energized by your mouthy misdeeds, and your soul is inflamed with hell. Abba Hyperechius said, "He who speaks against his neighbor will be like the serpent [in the Garden of Eden], for he corrupts the soul of him who listens to him and he does not save his own soul."[5] Our world is no better for your having spoken. Your tongue dealt death. And death is your reward.

A more subtle form of verbal death happens when we empty the meaning of words through sheer proliferation. Henri Nouwen suggested that the burgeoning of mass media has resulted in words losing their "creative power." To the biblical mind, the primary function of words is to create communion, to bring life. And yet the trivialization of our words has made it so that

> the main function of the word, which is communication, is no longer realized. The word no longer communicates, no longer fosters communion, no longer creates community, and therefore no longer gives life. The word no longer offers trustworthy ground on which people can meet each other and build society.[6]

Whether our speech is dramatically or subtly evil, the counsel that comes out of the desert is the same: We must learn to control our words. Before we learn to speak again, we must learn to be silent.

This is difficult in any age. But it is especially difficult now. In the era of Facebook, Twitter, YouTube, and Instagram, everyone has a megaphone. Sounding off on your pet topic is both easier and more rewarding than ever—just think of the "likes" you'll get! Add to this that we live in the age of self-actualization, where we've told people that everyone has an unconditional moral obligation to *express* themselves, that whatever is in your heart needs to come out of your mouth, that the world needs to hear what you have to say—and we've got the makings of a big social problem.

The net result is that we give constant expression to every foolish, self-justifying, incoherent, illogical, deviant, angry, lustful, envious, despicable, self-aggrandizing, malicious, contemptuous, murderous thought that pops into our heads. And what is worse, we tend to feel *good* about it. (At least for the moment. The time to pay the piper always comes.) Under the innocent banner of a supposedly harmless self-actualization, we torch our world with verbal napalm and, like fools, wonder why everything is burning down around us. Our arrogance is matched by our thickheadedness.

Jesus knew about our human tendency toward this. In his classic teaching on the way of the Kingdom, the Sermon on the Mount, he remarked:

> You have heard that it was said to the people long ago, "You shall not murder, and anyone who murders will be subject to judgment." But I tell you that anyone who is angry with a brother or sister will be subject to judgment. Again, anyone who says to a brother or sister, "Raca," is answerable to the court. And anyone who says, "You fool!" will be in danger of the fire of hell.
>
> MATTHEW 5:21-22

Jesus, as he characteristically does, refuses to address murder simply at the level of gross violence. He wants to go further back. Deeper down. He aims to pull the fruit of murder up by the root of our contempt for one another. *Raca* was an Aramaic term of contempt, as *fool* then and now is. And contempt is an annihilating emotion. Folks talk these days about "cancel culture." Contempt is one of the roots of that culture. It is everywhere, and it is deadly. The moment contempt seeps into relationships—between spouses, family members, employers and employees, political parties, social classes, ethnic groups—the death spiral has begun. A total overhaul is required. *Flee, be silent, pray always . . .*

Bluntly stated, the problem with our mouths is that our hearts are bad. "The mouth speaks what the heart is full of," said Jesus

(Luke 6:45). The many duplicities of the heart come rolling off the lips, poisoning God's good world. Jesus' half brother, James the Just, painted our situation with vivid colors:

> With the tongue we praise our Lord and Father, and with
> it we curse human beings, who have been made in God's
> likeness. Out of the same mouth come praise and cursing.
> My brothers and sisters, this should not be. Can both
> fresh water and salt water flow from the same spring? My
> brothers and sisters, can a fig tree bear olives, or a grapevine
> bear figs? Neither can a salt spring produce fresh water.
> JAMES 3:9-12

Blessings and curses flow from our lips in equal measure. And somehow the absurdity of it escapes us. We praise our Lord and Father, and we curse our fellow brothers and sisters, who have been made in God's image. We bless God, and we revile his living, breathing, walking images. Like saying the pledge of allegiance and then desecrating the flag. Like telling your wife you love her on your way out the door to work and then trashing her reputation to your colleagues. How much sense does that make? We can feel James' exasperation: *My brothers and sisters, this should not be!*

But such absurdity is what we should expect when we've surrendered control of our lives to our lips:

> When we put bits into the mouths of horses to make them
> obey us, we can turn the whole animal. Or take ships as
> an example. Although they are so large and are driven
> by strong winds, they are steered by a very small rudder
> wherever the pilot wants to go. Likewise, the tongue is a

small part of the body, but it makes great boasts. Consider
what a great forest is set on fire by a small spark. The
tongue also is a fire, a world of evil among the parts of the
body. It corrupts the whole body, sets the whole course of
one's life on fire, and is itself set on fire by hell.

JAMES 3:3-6

Bit and bridle steer the horse. Rudder steers the ship. Tongue
steers the life. Period.

MORTIFYING SPEECH

But James's words, if we are paying careful attention, raise a question: *Who steers the tongue?* It would be one thing if we simply had
a blind horse master or captain at the helm. In that case, a little
instruction might do the trick. For James, it's worse than all that.
The tongue "is itself set on fire by hell." When we surrender mastery
of our lips, the enemy of our souls is all too eager to take the reins.

Which is why, for the Desert Fathers and Mothers, the solution was so drastic. Radical diseases require radical remedies. Abba
Marcarius was dismissing some brothers from the assembly when
he said, "Flee, my brothers." Confused, one of them returned,
"Where could we flee to beyond this desert?" Macarius "put his
finger on his lips and said, 'Flee that.'"[7] You can try to change your
situation as the day is long, but unless you've changed your entire
relationship to the way you talk, you'll never be free.

Lest it escape our notice, such is the very nature of our salvation. Or at least so the Christian tradition has always taught. The
problem with human beings is not that we are misinformed and
need a little enlightenment; the problem is that we are enslaved to
sin. We need to be converted. We need to be brought from death

to life. To the Christian mind, *escape from death only occurs by death*. As Paul said, "We were therefore buried with him through baptism into death in order that, just as Christ was raised from the dead through the glory of the Father, we too may live a new life" (Romans 6:4).

"Buried with him through baptism and into death." *Mortification* is the old word for that. Like *mortal* or *mortality*, *mortification* is from the Latin root *mort*, which just means "death." Mortification occurs in us as the Spirit enables our consent to the death that alone liberates us—death with Christ.

This intuition illuminated the instincts of the desert. For instance, how do we keep from judging others? Abba Moses said that "the monk must die to his neighbour and never judge him at all, in any way whatever."[8] The reason that we judge our neighbors is that we—whether we realize it or not—are locked in a competitive relationship with them. We *need* to judge them to secure our own righteousness, or to protect ourselves. Turn on CNN or Fox News and witness the vitriol that ensues whenever a so-called panel of experts is summoned to weigh in on this or that issue. Rational, measured speech is abandoned at the first suggestion of disagreement. The need to prove the righteousness of one's cause, point of view, or position *over and against* that of our neighbor is the cause of so much verbal calamity.

And in any event, the knowledge of our own corruption leaves us little time or inclination to judge others. A brother asked Abba Moses, "What does [it] mean, to think in [your] heart that [a man] is a sinner?" Moses responded, "When someone is occupied with his own faults, he does not see those of his neighbor."[9] Moses' words call to mind the teaching of Jesus on judgments in Matthew 7. "You hypocrite," Jesus says, "first take the plank

STREAMS IN THE WASTELAND

out of your own eye, and then you will see clearly to remove the speck from your brother's eye" (Matthew 7:5). The plank just *is* our proclivity to see and judge others' unrighteousness and pay no attention to our own. Or, as Dallas Willard put it, "Condemnation *is* the board in our eye."[10] What madness. How can we be good physicians for others when we have not ourselves been cured?

Christians are in a unique position to get this right. Actually, we are, I think, in the *only* imaginable position to get it right. We, after all, are those who believe that Jesus Christ is the Word of the Father; the one definitive, truthful Word that has always and will always be spoken over and to humanity; the Word that gathers up all human words, weighs them in the scales, and finds them wanting. Our words have already-always been judged as *at least* woefully deficient—*at most* riddled with iniquity. The Word has come to save our words.

VIVIFYING SPEECH

In churches all over the world, week after week, Christians do something remarkable. They gather for worship. Worship, when it has not been reduced to entertainment, blasphemy, or banality, is saturated in the Word of God. The language of the Psalms and the Prophets, of Moses and David and Ezekiel and Jeremiah, of Paul and Peter and Matthew and John, makes up the form and content and pattern of our worship. We bring our human speech to the bar of the Word of God, by grace seeking to have our words match up to the great words of our faith.

It takes a little effort, but as the weeks and years go by, eventually we learn to speak life and not death; as the Word himself penetrates our ears and hearts, we acquire his dialect, we learn the cadences of the city of God.

There was a neat symmetry to how the ancients talked about this movement from the language of death to the language of life. *Mortification* was followed by *vivification*—the Spirit who unites us with the death of Christ also unites us with his life. We are endowed with life, imparted life, given life by the one who is called in the Nicene Creed "the Lord, the Giver of Life." Our old, corrupt frame is given new vitality, new impetus, new direction as by the Spirit we are made one in spirit and body with the Christ, whose whole life was and is directed to the Father. The Spirit will direct ours to the Father as well. Mouths that once poured out folly will slowly learn to bless and strengthen the world without hesitation or qualification—as Jesus did and does.

A great deal of this happens in worship. There—

- We learn to praise God—"Oh give thanks to the LORD; call upon his name; make known his deeds among the people!" (1 Chronicles 16:8, ESV).

- We learn to tell the truth about other human beings—"So God created mankind in his own image, in the image of God he created them; male and female he created them" (Genesis 1:27).

- We learn to bless and not curse—"The LORD bless you and keep you; the LORD make his face shine on you and be gracious to you; the LORD turn his face toward you and give you peace" (Numbers 6:24-26).

- And most of all, we learn how to *repent*. Perhaps there is no Christian act more radical than this—at least when it comes to our speech. Repentance is the *verbal* act by which we acknowledge that our whole way of being is out of sync with the Kingdom. By acknowledging that we *haven't* lived truthful lives, we finally *begin to live truthful lives.*

And so, gathered as the people of God, we say words that go something like this:

Most merciful God,
we confess that we have sinned against you
in thought, word, and deed,
by what we have done,
and by what we have left undone.
We have not loved you with our whole heart;
we have not loved our neighbors as ourselves.
We are truly sorry and we humbly repent.
For the sake of your Son Jesus Christ,
have mercy on us and forgive us;
that we may delight in your will,
and walk in your ways,
to the glory of your Name. Amen.[11]

The minister pronounces the good news of pardon over us. Perhaps a text like "If we confess our sins, he is faithful and just and will forgive us our sins and purify us from all unrighteousness" (1 John 1:9) or "Come to me all you who labor and are heavy laden, and I will give you rest" (Matthew 11:28, author's paraphrase). The Anglican tradition calls words such as these "the comfortable words." I like that. These words of comfort mediate to us the reality that Jesus Christ is the True Word of comfort and pardon. He is the Word more absolute than our failed and faulty words. As the minister speaks these words, we realize that the truest thing about us is merciful Jesus, and we are inspired to live mercifully, truthfully as a result.

Which means, in part, that we are liberated from the need to judge others with our words. Trusting Jesus Christ, the Righteous One, not only with our own lives but the lives of others, we can release them and speak blessing over them. As the Word mortifies and vivifies our words, we find that we are empowered to carry the healing word that he is and has to the world.

VERBAL PILGRIMAGE

They buried George Floyd in his hometown of Pearland, a suburb of Houston, Texas. June 9, 2020. Thousands came to witness one of the most public funerals in our nation's memory. George's death in Minneapolis two weeks prior had sparked national outrage. Four-hundred-and-fifty years' worth of hurt came rushing once again to the surface of our collective consciousness, demanding our attention. Emotions that had long smoldered suddenly ran hot. The fires of centuries-old debates were stoked once again. *What's really going on here? Who's to blame? How do we fix it?*

Fires burned in our cities too. While many gathered in prayer and in peaceful protest, and others raised their voices in righteous indignation, still others set to looting and rioting in the cities. Tumult from San Francisco to Atlanta, from Minneapolis to New Orleans. Folks in power struggled to respond. It was a tenuous national moment.

If ever there was a moment for incendiary words to be spoken, the Floyd funeral was it. But what was remarkable was that, according to reports, not an angry, vengeful, hateful word was uttered. No bitter invective against white supremacists (though it would have been justified). No angry diatribes decrying police brutality (however urgent and necessary that conversation). No threats of violence in the streets. Just gracious, hopeful speech.

Princeton professor emeritus Dr. Cornel West, in an interview with CNN's Anderson Cooper, related the spirit of the day:

> It was a heavy day, my brother. And yet, I was buoyed up because I saw in the hearts and minds and souls [of those in attendance] a love. Not one reference to hatred or revenge. It was all about love and justice. It's in the great tradition of the best of Black people, a people who have been hated chronically, systemically for four hundred years, but have taught the world so much about love. . . . After four hundred years of being terrorized, we *refuse* to create a Black version of the Ku Klux Klan. After four hundred years of being traumatized, we wanna dish out healers. . . . What is it about these Black people, so thoroughly subjugated, but want freedom for everybody? That's a grand gift to the world.[12]

Indeed it is. The interview brought Cooper to tears. It immediately went viral. A stunning reversal of expectations.

Let's be clear, here. There is a place for righteous indignation, for shrill denunciations, for fiery words. And the Scriptures invite us to see that such words can also be, and often are, a work of the Spirit. The prophets, after all, inspired by the Spirit, with the word of God in their hearts, rained down harangue upon God's people—particularly the rich and powerful among them—for their abuse and oppression of others. And our Lord Jesus Christ himself was no stranger to dishing out hard words against those who tied up heavy loads upon people's shoulders (Matthew 23:4).

Our God is the God who gives voice to the voiceless. He is and forever will be the God of the oppressed. He will not stifle or suppress their cry.

And yet here where we may have expected harangue, to the surprise of many, something else came out: words of grace and peace. But maybe we shouldn't have been so surprised. James Cone and others have argued that, at the center of much of the Black experience in the United States, sitting right next to—indeed, radiating through—the experience of racial injustice is a buoyant spirituality. A confidence in the person of Jesus Christ cascading through every era and experience of oppression, which has consistently awakened a *refuse-to-be-denied* kind of hope, a confidence that gave rise to folks like Dr. Martin Luther King Jr., whose words on racial healing and reconciliation still resound in our hearts. Speaking of the civil rights movement of the 1950s and 1960s, Cone writes, "The spirituals were the soul of the movement, giving people courage to fight, and the church was its anchor, deepening its faith in the coming freedom for all."[13]

To know Jesus, crucified and raised to life, is to know something about the destiny of the world that the world does not know, which enables us to speak in ways that both shock and delight. As we draw near to him, in worship and prayer and private devotion, we find that he heals our hearts—and our speech—and indeed, our entire lives. As we have heard Abba Nilus say, "Prayer is the seed of gentleness and the absence of anger."

How many times I have found this to be true. I'll come to God, burning hot with anger against my brother or my sister, willing my vindication (and sometimes their hurt)—only to find that the molten presence of our good God, the Word-made-flesh, Jesus Christ, melts my anger into a desire for peace. As my heart shifts in his presence, so also does my speech. I'm transformed. This is what is at the heart of Abba Pambo's words to Abba Theodore: "Theodore, go and have pity on all, for through pity, one finds freedom of speech before God."[14] When our hearts are soft, our speech is sound.

This is a crucial part of what makes the spirituality of the desert practical, and *practicable*, in our day and in our time. We don't need a change of location—we need a change of heart. The fathers and mothers insist on this. Abba Longinus said, "If you cannot control your tongue, you will not be an exile anywhere. Therefore, control your tongue here and you will be an exile."[15] Abba Tithoes said, "Pilgrimage means that a man should control his tongue."[16]

In the presence of Jesus Christ, we are enabled to make this pilgrimage. We can become exiles and aliens in the midst of the noisy, clamorous, cantankerous cities and villages in which we live. Living in the ebb and flow of his goodness, we will begin to know exactly when to be silent and exactly when to speak. We will live attending to his presence, knowing how to bring forth a word in due season. "A word fitly spoken," said the writer of Proverbs, "is like apples of gold in settings of silver" (Proverbs 25:11, KJ21). Our words will be fit for every occasion because our hearts have been fitted to the reality of God in Christ.

This is another critical insight about our speech that must not be lost. There is a kind of legalistic, supercilious silence that misses the spirit of what the fathers and mothers of the desert advocated. The Word must penetrate the depths, or our silence avails us nothing. "A man may seem to be silent," said Abba Poemen, "but if his heart is condemning others he is babbling ceaselessly. But there may be another who talks from morning till night and yet he is truly silent; *that is, he says nothing that is not profitable*."[17] Richard

Foster relates, "Simply to refrain from talking, without a heart listening to God, is not silence."[18]

The *heart* of silence is the *pure heart* that knows what to say and when to say it. A person with such a heart not only can *safely* speak—but *should speak*. As Poemen instructed, "Teach your mouth to say that which you have in your heart."[19] Such a heart has been made a temple of the Holy Spirit, a shelter and a shade for the Word, who heals and brings life.

Such a heart knows also that under the right conditions, *even silence speaks a word that edifies*. Isidore of Pelusia said, "To live without speaking is better than to speak without living. For the former who lives rightly does good even by his silence but the latter does no good even when he speaks."[20] Williams writes that "there is a silence that is poisonous and evil"—such as the silence that comes when we have been muted by others, when we refuse to speak up on behalf of others, or when we refuse to offer hospitality and grace with our words. On the other hand, he writes, "There is an affirming silence that is attentive, focused, and that comes out of peace, not anger, from fullness, not woundedness."[21] Perhaps you've been the recipient of this kind of silence—the kind that respects you, receiving your presence and your hope and your vexation as a sacred mystery, as a token of the divine presence. Silence like that is, in its own way, a word that brings life.

But better even than living without speaking is knowing *when* to speak: "When words and life correspond to one another," Isidore went on, "they are together the whole of philosophy."[22]

What does it take to live this way? It's not easy, but it is simple. We'll have to keep rigorously submitting ourselves to Jesus Christ. Remember what was said of Abba John the Dwarf: "When he returned from the harvest or when he had been with some of the old men, he gave himself to prayer, meditation and psalmody until his thoughts were re-established in their previous order."

Only by the disciplines of silence, solitude, and prayer can we hope to have our speech transformed. Only a people submitted to the Word, Jesus Christ, can hope to bring a healing word to the world.

CHAPTER 8

SANCTIFYING WORK

*The LORD God took the man and put him in the
Garden of Eden to work it and take care of it.*
GENESIS 2:15

*If Moses had not led his sheep to Midian,
he would not have seen him who was in the bush.*
ABBA POEMEN

MY DAD, WILLIAM JAMES ARNDT, is the most excellent man I know.

I've joked sometimes that it's a bit annoying. Do you have any idea how impossible the standard is for the oldest son (me) of a man like this? Seriously. How can a person be good at literally *everything* he attempts to do? Maybe it's his Boy Scout background. Or maybe he's just made out of different "stuff" than the rest of us. I don't know.

But truly, he's good at everything. It amazed me as a kid. Sports? *Check.* He played pickup basketball three times a week for years over the lunch hour with his friends and typically dominated the floor. Serving the church? *Check.* He leveraged his background in theater to lead worship on a regular basis for our congregation, even singing "O Come, O Come Emmanuel" a cappella one Advent as a special—a gutsy move, which he (big surprise) nailed. Home improvement and repair? *Check.* He once built a bathroom in our basement in his spare time (he regularly worked fifty to sixty hours a week at his normal job) in less than three weeks. Gardening? *Check.* In the summer, my parents' Wisconsin backyard, with its lush green grass and multiple vegetable and flower gardens that annually explode with abundance, makes the Shire look like an abandoned Walmart parking lot.

Oh, and here's one that was super annoying: video games. Again—*check.* When we bought our first Nintendo back in the 1980s, my dad popped in *The Legend of Zelda* cartridge, beat it in one sitting, and promptly retired from playing video games ever again. True story. The Bobby Fischer of Nintendo.

Did I mention my dad is fit and handsome too?

But seriously, everything my dad puts his hand to do, he excels in. His job was one such area. He caught on as a salesman at a fledgling, family-owned car dealership in Marshfield before I was born and, as the years went by, worked his way up through the ranks. A top salesman every year, he went on to manage various areas and departments of the dealership before eventually becoming the general manager.

Under his leadership, the dealership thrived, posting record sales year after year, eventually building a beautiful state-of-the-art facility where my dad and his team of salesmen put folks not just in our community but across the state (and beyond) in new and used vehicles that exactly fit their needs, providing them with excellent service along the way. Even now, living in Colorado, every once in a while I'll see a car with a "V&H Autos" sticker on the back, or an eighteen-wheeler with "V&H" mud flaps, and I'll smile. *An Arndt helped do that*, I'll think.

My dad worked that job for nearly forty years (he retired in 2019). Day in and day out, through sometimes excruciatingly long days and difficult seasons, his efforts built up a thriving enterprise that brought great dignity and value to a lot of people's lives.

One time, maybe ten or so years ago, he and I were on a run together on a gorgeous Wisconsin summer day, and we got to talking about his career. In the middle of the conversation, he remarked, "Sometimes it's difficult for me to see the value of what I've done in terms of the Kingdom. Every now and again, I wonder if my efforts would have had a greater impact if I had directed them elsewhere."

That remark stopped me cold. As a witness to my dad's life, the "Kingdom" impact of his work was (and is) so evident to me. From the benefit it brought to the family who owned the dealership and trusted him like Pharoah trusted Joseph; to the hundreds of people who worked with and for my dad who were blessed and built up

STREAMS IN THE WASTELAND

by his leadership; to the thousands of families and individuals who were served by getting good deals on cars that fit their needs without the stress of haggling . . . the impact is staggering. And that's not saying *anything* yet about the *economic* impact to the region of having this dealership thrive; nor of the fact that for nearly forty years this job was a predictable, stable, growing financial cornerstone for the Arndt family, which also allowed my parents to be incredibly generous to our church; nor of the fact that it provided a place where my dad's energies and abilities could find fruitful, creative expression as they developed—a context where he could become so much of who God designed him to be.

I shared some of those things with him that day on the run. It was a fun and illuminating conversation for both of us. And it got me thinking more deeply about the role of the work of our hands as an expression of who we are as citizens of the Kingdom—of human labor as a crucial environment for the embodiment of holiness in the world.

Of that, the desert has much to teach us.

SAVED BY ROPE MAKING

Once again, we tend to think of the Desert Fathers and Mothers as purely preoccupied with "spiritual matters" like prayer and solitude and Bible reading—that they are folks who have little or nothing to do with the more mundane matters of everyday life. But a visit to the cell of the average abba or amma would quickly put that notion to rest. They saw ordinary work as central to the life of the Kingdom. Consider this story of Abba Anthony:

> When the holy Abba Anthony lived in the desert he
> was beset by *accidie* [I'll define this in a moment], and

attacked by many sinful thoughts. He said to God, "Lord, I want to be saved but these thoughts do not leave me alone; what shall I do in my affliction? How can I be saved?" A short while afterwards, when he got up to go out, Anthony saw a man like himself sitting at his work, getting up from his work to pray, then sitting down and plaiting a rope, then getting up again to pray. It was an angel of the Lord sent to correct and reassure him. He heard the angel saying to him, "Do this and you will be saved." At these words, Anthony was filled with joy and courage. He did this, and he was saved.[1]

Pay careful attention to what is going on here. We don't talk much about "accidie" (or "acedia") anymore, but the ancient church—and the Desert Fathers and Mothers in particular—saw it as a primary and rather vicious spiritual foe. In fact, Abba Poemen, who we've met before, remarked that "there is no worse passion" than *accidie* and gave specific counsel on how to root it out.[2] But what is it?

Benedicta Ward defines *accidie* as "despondency, depression, listlessness, a distaste for life without any specific reason."[3] The third-century Desert Father Evagrius Ponticus characterized it as "the noonday devil" for the way in which it tended to (and still tends to) hit people right in the middle of the day, as they are carrying out their ordinary tasks and responsibilities.

You know the feeling. You wake up in the morning, get yourself geared up for the challenge of the day, plunge into your tasks and responsibilities with vigor, put in a few good hours of work, stop for a lunch break, return to your work . . . *and then it hits.* Somewhere around 1:30 or 2:00 p.m. You're back at it: staring at a computer screen, walking the showroom floor, looking at a half-cleaned house, contemplating the stack of books that you have to somehow turn into a term paper . . . and all you can think to do is to watch funny videos of cats on Facebook or just take a nap. *Did I pick the wrong career?* you ask yourself. *Wouldn't I be happier if. . . ?* you muse. *Why am I so tired . . . ?* you wonder. *Maybe I have mono. Or chronic fatigue syndrome. Or just need a vacation. But wait—I just got back from vacation. Is it too soon to take another one . . . ?*

Before long, if you're not careful, the thoughts become darker. *What is the point of what I'm doing?* you wonder. *Does my life have any purpose?* An atmosphere of gray and stifling sadness slowly descends. *My marriage is lame. Parenting is such a chore. I don't like my church. I don't like my friends. I don't like myself. I need to move far away from here.* Psalm 55:6 suddenly becomes your life verse: "If only I had wings like a dove! I would fly away and find rest" (CSB).

So you check out of work early, chalking your departure up to a stomachache or a headache or just an *anything-ache*, and you head home, only to find your time back at the house as empty and wearying as your time at the office. What in the world is wrong?

The Desert Fathers and Mothers would say, "You are under assault from an ancient foe—the noonday devil of *accidie*." It attacks disciples now in much the same way that it did back then. John Cassian described the assault of *accidie* on a monk like this:

> He fancies that he will never be well while he stays in that place, unless he leaves his cell . . . . Then the fifth or sixth hour brings him such bodily weariness and longing for food that he seems to himself worn out and wearied . . . Then besides this he looks about anxiously this way and

that, and sighs that none of the brethren come to see him, and often goes in and out of his cell, and frequently gazes up at the sun, as if it was too slow in setting, and so a kind of unreasonable confusion of mind takes possession of him like some foul darkness, and makes him idle and useless for every spiritual work, so that he imagines that no cure for so terrible an attack can be found in anything except visiting some one of the brethren, or in the solace of sleep alone.[4]

In other words, feeling purposeless and futile, the monk wanders about in a kind of spiritual fog that manifests as purposeless and futile activity, opening his mind and soul up to further attacks by the noonday devil. *Accidie* not only takes the monk away from productive labor (thwarting a crucial flow of life through him) but also damages his spirit. Both dimensions of *accidie's* attack are critical to understand.

So what is to be done? How do we escape this vicious spiritual vortex?

ORA ET LABORA

That is precisely the question that Anthony was wrestling with when he saw the vision of "a man like himself," which turned out to be an angel coming to "correct and reassure him." What was the angel doing? Nothing more or less complicated than engaging in a rhythm of meaningful (if simple) work and prayer. The angel promises that Anthony's dark and disturbing thoughts will subside and finally recede entirely if he gives himself to a life characterized by such a rhythm. He does and is saved.

The story illustrates that work and prayer *together* lead to a life of salvation, of gospel wholeness. Saint Benedict of Nursia, the late fifth- and early sixth-century Italian monk and "father of Western monasticism," took the insights of the Desert Fathers and Mothers (via John Cassian) on this point and built his entire vision of the monastic life around it. The cornerstone of "The Rule of Saint Benedict"—a set of guidelines to order monastic life—is (in Latin): *ora et labora* and *pax*. In answer to the question, "How do we live meaningfully and deeply together in the salvation that God has created for us in Christ Jesus?" Benedict answers, with the Desert Fathers and Mothers: *Ora et labora* ("work and prayer") with the result being *pax* ("peace"). That is, if we undertake the responsibilities of our lives with prayerful diligence, God's *shalom*, his wholeness, will steal not only into our lives but into the world around us.

As ever, the Desert Fathers and Mothers refuse to let spirituality drift off into the ether. They bless neither the excesses of narcissistic, self-infatuated introspection nor quasi-gnostic mystical flights into the sublime. A funny story from early in the life of the great Abba John the Dwarf that illustrates this:

> It was said of Abba John the Dwarf, that one day he said to his elder brother, "I should like to be free of all care, like the angels, who do not work, but ceaselessly offer worship to God." So he took off his cloak and went away into the desert. After a week he came back to his brother. When he knocked on the door, he heard his brother say, before he opened it, "Who are you?" He said, "I am John, your brother." But he replied, "John has become an angel, and henceforth he is no longer among men." Then the other begged him, saying, "It is I." However, his

brother did not let him in, but left him there in distress until morning. Then, opening the door, he said to him, "You are a man and you must once again work in order to eat." Then John made a prostration before him, saying, "Forgive me."[5]

The Desert Fathers and Mothers keep the feet of our spirituality firmly on the ground: planted in the dirt; attuned to the conditions of our creatureliness; nailed down to the ordinary rhythms of waking and sleeping, eating and drinking, working and resting and playing—and all of it saturated with reverent God-awareness. They call us *both* to plaiting ropes *and* to praying; *both* to running kids to and from school *and* to ruminating on the things of God; *both* to mowing the grass *and* to meditating on Scripture; *both* to cleaning the house *and* to cleansing our spirits. And in this they mirror a central concern of the Scriptures.

THE BIBLE AND WORK

Right from the outset, the Bible underscores the value of human work. In the account of Creation found in Genesis 2, we read this:

No shrub had yet appeared on the earth and no plant had yet sprung up, for the LORD God had not sent rain on the earth and there was no one to work the ground, but streams came up from the earth and watered the whole surface of the ground. Then the LORD God formed a man from the dust of the ground and breathed into his nostrils the breath of life, and the man became a living being.

Now the LORD God had planted a garden in the east, in Eden; and there he put the man he had formed.

The LORD God made all kinds of trees grow out of the ground—trees that were pleasing to the eye and good for food. In the middle of the garden were the tree of life and the tree of the knowledge of good and evil. . . .

The LORD God took the man and put him in the Garden of Eden to work it and take care of it.

GENESIS 2:5-8, 15

There are a few critical things to notice about this text. First, notice that it affixes the question of what God is doing with human beings right *inside* the created order. There is no suggestion that God's purposes for us lie anywhere outside of this created realm.

Second, pushing that first point a bit further, notice that human beings share an ongoing and organic relationship with their environment. The Hebrew word for "ground" here is *adamah*, while the Hebrew word for "man" is *adam*. The *adam* is drawn from the *adamah*—the only difference being that *adam* is given a unique share of the divine life (God breathes into this bit of ground) and is stamped with the divine image (Genesis 1). But as far as the "stuff" that *adam* is made out of—it is always and forever the *adamah*, which he will need to continually draw from to survive. This is why the Hebrew writer underscores the presence of the trees that grow up from the *adamah*, which bear fruit to feed the *adam*. We always exist as a living, organic part of our environment. We need it to survive.

One final thing to notice: Humans have been given a divine commission regarding their environment. The Lord places them inside the Garden of Eden for a purpose: "to work it and take care of it."

Now this is an interesting phrase. The Hebrew words for "work it" and "take care of it" are *abad* and *shamar*, respectively. "Work" and "take care" are decent enough translations, but I think a better take on them might be "cultivate" and "protect." *Abad* really is about how we draw the latent potential out of a thing, while *shamar* is about how we protect or "keep" a thing from malign influences.

So what was the core vocation of *adam*? It was to partner with God in helping Eden become all that God desired it to be through creative work. You might recall that while the *beginning* of the story of Scripture is a garden paradise, the *end* of the biblical story is a garden *city*: the new Jerusalem (Revelation 21–22). The message is clear: Human beings are called to develop creation (and ourselves) to its fullest potential, and *work* is how we do that—which, by the way, is the problem with *accidie*: it severs us from that purpose.

Understanding this helps ward off the common misunderstanding that work is the result of the Fall. Certainly our work has been *impacted* by the Fall, a fact Genesis itself draws attention to. But what we have here in Genesis 2 is a commission *before* the Fall to cultivate and keep the created order. Indeed, the call to creative, productive labor is part of what it means to be made in the image and likeness of God (Genesis 1:26-27). Think about how the book of Genesis opens: *In the beginning God created the heavens and the earth*. The very first verb used to talk about God in the Hebrew Scriptures is a word (*bārā'*—"to create") that depicts *God at creative, productive work amid the created order*. And therefore, to be made in his image and likeness is to do the same—and more than that, it is to join with Creator God in the building up of his world.

THE SACREDNESS OF WORK

The Scriptures never cast aspersion on the ordinary work of our hands because when human labor is functioning as it should, God's purposes come to bear upon the world through it and God's glory is revealed in it. Let me give you a couple examples of what I mean.

Years ago, I pastored a church that had as one of its stated core values "the sacredness of work." We talked often and enthusiastically about how the mission of God goes forward in the world through the work of our hands. Over time, it became both a powerful discipleship tool for us as well as a powerful statement of where our priorities lay as a church—not only in the building up of the body but also in the equipping and "sending" of the members of the body into their various callings in the world.

One day, I grabbed lunch with one of our congregants, David, who at the time worked in urban planning and design. I was curious about his vocational journey—how he wound up in his field, what his job involved, what motivated him, and how he connected it all to the life of the Kingdom. He told me about his background in the arts and about his passion for the Bible's vision of a world marked by *shalom*—the universal flourishing of all people and all things. For David, given both his ability and his convictions, the natural occupational path was urban planning and design. He could spend his days dreaming about and creating plans for the development of neighborhoods that, by their design, would stimulate the flourishing of the people in them—with walkways and bike paths and open areas and playgrounds all designed to get people outdoors (promoting health) and interacting with one another (promoting community). His efforts are contributing to the blessing and building up of the world. *Abad* and *shamar*.

Too often, the way that we talk about the value of work in

the church reduces it to a mere instrumentality. "Work is sacred," we tell people, "when it is specifically 'religious' work. Preaching or teaching or leading worship or doing overseas mission trips. If you can't do those things, at least try to do something that's not evil and that earns you a decent wage so that you can contribute financially to the church."

"Hogwash," I say—and the Desert Fathers and Mothers would agree. "Church" work is not more holy than any other kind of work. It is *the spirit* in which we undertake our labors, and the ends to which those labors are directed, that render them holy or not: "It was revealed to Abba Anthony in his desert that there was one who was his equal in the city. He was a doctor by profession and whatever he had beyond his needs he gave to the poor, and every day he sang the Sanctus with the angels."[6]

Do you see it? Doctoring is a needed profession, and this doctor was practicing it in the spirit of *ora et labora*, with *pax* being the result.

The English poet and novelist Dorothy Sayers, in a brilliant essay on the meaning and dignity of human work, remarked that "Christian people, and particularly perhaps the Christian clergy, must get it firmly into their heads that when a man or woman is called to a particular job of secular work, that is as true a vocation as though he or she were called to specifically religious work." Then she identified the devastating effects of *not* doing this:

> In nothing has the Church so lost Her hold on reality
> as in Her failure to understand and respect the secular
> vocation. She has allowed work and religion to become
> separate departments, and is astonished to find that, as
> result, the secular work of the world is turned to purely

selfish and destructive ends, and that the greater part of
the world's intelligent workers have become irreligious, or
at least, uninterested in religion.

But is it astonishing? How can any one remain
interested in a religion which seems to have no concern
with nine-tenths of his life? The Church's approach to an
intelligent carpenter is usually confined to exhorting him
not to be drunk and disorderly in his leisure hours, and
to come to church on Sundays. What the Church should
be telling him is this: that the very first demand that his
religion makes upon him is that he should make good
tables.[7]

Faith in the Incarnate God refuses to surrender any part of our
lived existence to the evil one. And yet, when we fail to appreciate
the full meaning of human labor in the plan of God, we tacitly do
exactly that—with tragic results: "The secular work of the world
is turned to purely selfish and destructive ends."

We need to do better. We need to reclaim the intrinsic holiness
of our work, bringing its sacred depths to visibility as we seek God
and the good of others in it, understanding it as an expression
of the many ways that God is working to bless and build up his
world. "Teach me work," writes Wendell Berry, "that honors Thy
work."[8] And what is "Thy work"? *Whatever God is doing to bring
his* shalom—*"thy Kingdom come, thy will be done, on earth as it is
in heaven"—to bear on his world.*

FOR THE SAKE OF THE WORLD

In one of Berry's finest stories, *Jayber Crow*, the title character thinks
he may be called to the ministry and receives a scholarship to become

a pre-ministerial student at nearby Pigeonville College. But in the midst of his studies, Jayber begins to be troubled by some personal doubts, which he expresses to a teacher, Dr. Ardmire. He and Dr. Ardmire both agree that the doubts are significant enough to disqualify him from any further pursuit of ministry as an occupational path.

Discouraged, Jayber says to Dr. Ardmire, "I had this feeling maybe I had been called." Dr. Ardmire (astutely) responds, "And you may have been right. But not to what you thought. Not to what you think."[9] Jayber departs from Pigeonville College into a life as a barber at the small town of Port William, where for decades his barbershop will serve as a crucial place for the building up and blessing of human lives and the nurturing of community. Called? Yes indeed. *But not to what he thought.* He was called *into the world for the sake of the world.*

Human beings are called to enter God's efforts to bring his Kingdom and accomplish his will in the world through the work of their hands. My friend Ronnie, for example, works as a neurosurgeon. People facing life-and-death scenarios come to him for his expert advice and skill. And every single day, his efforts preserve and bless human life. *Thy Kingdom come; thy will be done.*

My friends Rich and Becky have recently opened a beautiful group home where adults with special needs can come and live in community with caretakers who live in the residence with them, so that they don't become wards of the state and get lost in the system. *Thy Kingdom come; thy will be done.*

My friend Mark runs a counseling practice here in town that serves thousands of clients, offering everything from routine marital maintenance to treatment for folks struggling with more serious psychological disorders, leading them along paths of well-being and wholeness. *Thy Kingdom come; thy will be done.*

My sister, Anna, has worked in public schools for many years as both a teacher and an administrator, serving mostly in under-resourced communities where many of the kids lack support at home. Despite many obstacles, she presses on because the kids are worth it. *Thy Kingdom come; thy will be done.*

And that's saying nothing about the "behind the scenes" labors that we all engage in—the work that keeps the world spinning and have nothing to do with a "job," per se. Paying the bills and washing clothes and cooking meals. Running kids between dance and youth group and school. Creating moments around the kitchen table for discipleship and spiritual formation. Shoveling the driveway for retired neighbors. Inviting people who have nowhere else to go to a holiday brunch. *Thy Kingdom come; thy will be done.*

SANCTIFYING WORK

And now, as we see work as it is meant to be, we can better understand what the Lord said to Adam after Adam and Eve made the fateful choice to eat from the tree of the knowledge of good and evil:

> Because you listened to your wife and ate fruit from the tree about which I commanded you, "You must not eat from it,"
>
> Cursed is the ground because of you;
>> through painful toil you will eat food from it
>> all the days of your life.
> It will produce thorns and thistles for you,
>> and you will eat the plants of the field.

By the sweat of your brow
    you will eat your food
until you return to the ground,
    since from it you were taken;
for dust you are
    and to dust you will return.

GENESIS 3:17-20

The Fall did not *create* work. God created work and created it to be good—for us and for the world. What the Fall did was *distort* and *warp* and *frustrate* work.

Ponder for just a moment, and you'll begin to see that many of the great problems of our world are a product of distorted, warped work—that is, work driven along by sin. It is a *good thing* that we have folks like my friend David who are thinking carefully about the design of neighborhoods; it is a *bad thing* that we have others who are only thinking about how to cheaply build as much living space as possible in the smallest amount of square footage possible while charging as much as possible. It is a *good thing* that we have folks like my friend Ronnie who are fighting daily for the well-being of their patients; it is a *bad thing* that we have people working in the health care industry who profit from keeping patients perpetually sick and medicated. It is a *good thing* that we have people like Rich and Becky who are working hard for those who might become victims of a soulless system; it is a *bad thing* that we have others who are doing all they can to prop up and benefit from that system.

Work driven by sin perverts God's good world. By the same token, work driven by the Spirit of God sanctifies and restores God's good world. It is part and parcel of the mission of God to make right all that has been made wrong by sin. Which is why Paul says bluntly:

> Whatever you do, work at it with all your heart, as working for the Lord, not for human masters, since you know that you will receive an inheritance from the Lord as a reward. It is the Lord Christ you are serving.
> COLOSSIANS 3:23-24

For Paul, human labor is part of how we express and actualize the fact that our lives are "hidden with Christ in God" (Colossians 3:3). Work guided by the Spirit of God is "sanctifying work," and we can throw ourselves into it wholeheartedly.

I'm using the phrase "sanctifying work" in two distinct but related ways that correspond to the "creational" purpose of work. A story of Abba Lucius illustrates the distinction:

> Some of the monks who are called Euchites went to Enaton to see Abba Lucius. The old man asked them, "What is your manual work?" They said, "We do not touch manual work but as the Apostle says, we pray without ceasing." The old man asked them if they did not eat and they replied they did. So he said to them, "When you are eating, who prays for you then?" Again he asked them if they did not sleep and they replied they did. And he said to them, "When you are asleep, who prays for you then?" They could not find any answer to give him.
>
> He said to them, "Forgive me, but you do not act as you speak. I will show you how, while doing my manual work, I pray without interruption. I sit down with God,

soaking my reeds and plaiting my ropes, and I say, 'God, have mercy on me; according to your great goodness and according to the multitude of your mercies, save me from my sins.'" So he asked them if this were not prayer and they replied it was. Then he said to them, "So when I have spent the whole day working and praying, making thirteen pieces of money more or less, I put two pieces of money outside the door and I pay for my food with the rest of the money. He who takes the two pieces of money prays for me when I am eating and when I am sleeping; so, by the grace of God, I fulfill the precept to pray without ceasing."[10]

Lucius's counsel helps us understand that work is "sanctifying" to the extent that, through it, *we* are sanctified. His daily task of rope making is where he lives out the call to "pray without ceasing" (1 Thessalonians 5:17, KJV), asking God to purify him as he does his work.

Good, hard, honest labor does all the right things to us. It provides us with a natural structure of self-discipline that orders our days, weeks, months, and years. It calls us into relationships where we are accountable for our behavior and where we have to deal with the ordinary joys and frustrations of sharing a common goal with others whose flaws and shortcomings we have to daily put up with. It also teaches us the value of perseverance amid discouragement and drudgery.

In addition, by doing all these things (and more), work *exposes the condition of our souls.* Our formation (or lack thereof) is put on display in work. As we learn to submit ourselves to and rely on God in our work, we become, as Pope John Paul II once said, "more a human being"[11]—we more fully live into our nature as creatures made in the image and likeness of God. This is what I was driving at in our earlier story of Anthony I—in an important sense, through prayerful work, God's salvation comes to us. As Abba Poemen put it, "If Moses had not led his sheep to Midian, he would not have seen him who was in the bush"—that is, the sanctifying encounter with the living God is built into our work.[12]

Another thing Lucius helps us see is that, when we work in this way, we achieve not only a *sanctification of the worker and the work* but also *a sanctification of the world.* As Lucius works and prays, he is creating something of value for others (the ropes are sold in the market to someone who *needs* ropes), and he is earning money that can be a blessing to the poor. And so God's grace comes not just to the worker but to the world.

God's plans for humanity are realized and his glory is made manifest as we do our work in the Pauline spirit of "with all your heart, as working for the Lord." John Paul II aptly said that "work is a participation in God's activity" whereby "while providing the substance of life for themselves and their families" men and women *also* are "unfolding the Creator's work . . . and contributing by their personal industry to the realization in history of the divine plan."[13]

And the world *is* watching our work. Historian Alan Kreider has persuasively argued that one of the ways pagans were won into the early church was through the manner in which Christians conducted business. He quotes Justin Martyr, who routinely exhorted the first Christians to conduct themselves publicly in such a way that through their "patience and meekness . . . all men [would be drawn] from shame and evil desires." Justin, writing to pagans in defense of the gospel, goes on:

This we can show in the case of many who were once
on your side but have turned from the ways of violence
and tyranny overcome by observing the consistent lives
of their neighbors, or noting the strange patience of their
injured acquaintances, or experiencing the way they did
business with them.[14]

For Justin, folks being won over to the Kingdom through the
business practices of the church was routine and commonplace.
God, by his Spirit, was persuading people to repentance and faith
in Jesus not through tent meetings and evangelistic crusades but
through *business*.

Which should serve as a provocation and reminder to us: Our
work, whatever it is, matters. For not only is God sanctifying *us*
through it, but through it he is also sanctifying and saving the
world.

CHAPTER 9

DIVINE GENEROSITY

For God so loved the world that he gave his one and only Son.
JOHN 3:16

Look, and look again.
This world is not just a little thrill for the eyes.
It's more than bones.
It's more than the delicate wrist with its personal pulse.
It's more than the beating of a single heart.
It's praising.
It's giving until the giving feels like receiving.
MARY OLIVER

Abba Theodore of Pherme had acquired three good books. He came to
Abba Macarius and said to him, "I have three excellent books from which
I derive profit; the brethren also make use of them and derive profit from
them. Tell me what I ought to do: keep them for my use and that of the
brethren, or sell them and give the money to the poor?" The old man
answered him in this way, "Your actions are good; but it is best
of all to possess nothing." Hearing that, he went and sold his
books and gave the money for them to the poor.
AS TOLD IN *THE SAYINGS OF THE DESERT FATHERS*

N OT LONG AGO, I did a funeral for the sister of one of my colleagues. The young woman, whom I did not know, was only twenty-nine years old when she died in a tragic accident. She departed this life far too early.

Sitting with her family to discuss funeral preparations, right from the start I began to get a sense of who she was—a buoyant, big-hearted, larger-than-life figure whose presence blessed and strengthened everyone she touched. After we had discussed some preliminary matters, I began to ask them to tell me about her. The words her family used painted a compelling picture of a life well lived:

She had a great sense of humor . . .

Funny . . .

She was the best storyteller . . .

I immediately thought, *This is a person I'd want to be friends with*, and smiled. The descriptors kept rolling:

She was hardworking . . .

She didn't fall in with the crowd . . .

She was wild and fun . . .

I started to think of my own sister, Anna—of whom these things are also true—and that did it for me. As the picture they painted began to grow in color and clarity, I sensed a growing familiarity in my own heart for this young woman, and tears begin to wet the corner of my eyes. They kept going:

She was so loving . . .

She was protective . . .

She went out of her way to make others happy . . .

Now the tears were streaming down my face. More adjectives followed:

She was loyal . . .

She was incredibly generous . . .
Her mother finished by saying:
She was a delight . . .

The funeral itself was one of the most beautiful and emotional services—of any kind—that I've witnessed. Family member after family member shared of the impact of her life—her joy, her love, her large-heartedness, her generosity of spirit. I cried the entire time.

And walked away with fresh perspective on the question of what is it that makes a life poignant, what makes it "delightful."

All of us want to count. We want to make a difference. We want our lives to matter. But I think—in our time perhaps more than at any other time—we have no idea how that works. We have lost the secret of life—if indeed we ever had it.

We live now in an *American Idol* culture that says that the way to make your life count is to do everything you can to fight for your place, to stand out in the crowd, to make a name for yourself. And that is what we do. We spend all our energy on it. And we are constantly frustrated that life—despite our best attempts to achieve a sense of significance—feels empty. Even those among us who make it to the big stage will often complain about how elusive a sense of significance is.

I think what we do not realize is that we have gotten things exactly backward. Our modern attempts to secure significance, to make our lives count, are fundamentally wrongheaded because they are fundamentally me-centered, and therefore they obscure the most elemental structures of being, the most obvious and basic truths about life itself—truths that are manifest everywhere, if we only have eyes to see them.

Here we come to the final dimension of the desert's witness

to the redeemed life, one which I believe represents not only the full flowering of their spiritual vision but indeed the full flowering of the very life of the Spirit in our midst: the life of radical generosity.

BEST OF ALL

You can't read the Desert Fathers and Mothers without being profoundly struck by their attitude toward possessions. It is fair to say that they saw possessions as (at least) a distraction and (at most) a potentially deadly hindrance to life in the Kingdom, so they sought to live as lightly and simply as possible. Macarius's words from the beginning of this chapter summarize that attitude nicely: "Your actions are good; *but it is best of all to possess nothing.*" Upon hearing this, Theodore "sold his books and gave the money for them to the poor."[1]

Moments like this are everywhere in the desert tradition. As the men and women of the desert divested themselves of unnecessary possessions, they saw themselves embodying the invitation of Jesus to the rich young man in the Gospel of Matthew: "If you want to be perfect, go, sell your possessions and give to the poor, and you will have treasure in heaven. Then come, follow me" (Matthew 19:21)—which of course the young man finds difficult and so departs in sorrow. The disciples, shaken a bit by what they have seen, ask, "Who then can be saved?" (Matthew 19:25). Jesus replies that "with man this is impossible, but with God all things are possible" (Matthew 19:26). The implication is clear: Only with the help of God can we be free *from* slavery to possessions *for* the life of the Kingdom.

This kind of attitude, again, is characteristic of the desert—and we who live in a wealthy, acquisitive, and increasingly consumptive society would do well to pay attention to it. Their posture toward possessions stands as a prophetic rebuke to the vision of "the good life" commonly peddled today:

> Abba Agathon was walking with his disciples. One of them, finding a small green pea on the road, said to the old man, "Father, may I take it?" The old man, looking at him with astonishment, said, "Was it you who put it there?" "No," replied the brother. "How then," continued the old man, "can you take up something which you did not put down?"[2]

However inconsequential a small pea on the side of the road may *seem* to be, Agathon sees what is really at stake: *If you don't need it, and it wasn't yours to begin with—why burden yourself with it?* The wise writer of Ecclesiastes would agree: "Better one handful with tranquillity than two handfuls with toil and chasing after the wind" (Ecclesiastes 4:6).

How many of us spend our days in the pursuit and acquisition of what we *don't* have . . . when we *already* have all that we need? The Desert Fathers and Mothers challenge us by unmasking the illusion that having *more* will make us happy. They recall us constantly to the beauty of the life of simplicity characterized so brilliantly by the writer of Proverbs:

> Two things I ask of you, LORD;
>   do not refuse me before I die:
> Keep falsehood and lies far from me;
>   give me neither poverty nor riches,
>   but give me only my daily bread.

Otherwise, I may have too much and disown you
    and say, "Who is the LORD?"
Or I may become poor and steal,
    and so dishonor the name of my God.

PROVERBS 30:7-9

This sentiment, moreover, is embodied by Jesus, who taught us to pray "this day" (stipulating the "when") for "daily bread" (stipulating the amount; Matthew 6:11). We are called to ask neither for tomorrow's bread today nor for more than we would need in a given day. And the promise is that if we seek the Kingdom of God and his righteousness in and above all things, we'll find that everything we *really* need will always be there for us, right when we need it (Matthew 6:31-34). So, here again, the radicality of the desert witness draws our attention to the characteristics of the here-and-now Kingdom life.

HOW QUARRELS HAPPEN

But there is more. The Desert Fathers and Mothers are also deeply aware of how the desire to possess what God has not given us can *divide* us from one another:

Two hermits lived together for many years without a quarrel. One said to the other, "Let's have a quarrel with each other, as other men do." The other answered, "I don't know how a quarrel happens." The first said, "Look here, I put a brick between us, and I say, 'That's mine!' Then you say, 'No, it's mine!' That is how you begin a quarrel." So they put a brick between them and one of them said, "That's mine!" The other said, "No, it's mine!"

The first answered, "Yes, it is yours. Take it away." So they were unable to argue with each other.[3]

Humorous as it is, the story makes a crucial point. What is at stake in the attitude of the Desert Fathers and Mothers toward possessions is not only the beauty of a life of simplicity but the desire to strike a blow at one of the deepest threats to the human race—the sin of envy. Remember the story of Cain and Abel (Genesis 4)? Cain *envied* the praise that Abel received from the Lord, and—believing that *more* for Abel meant *less* for him—murdered his brother.

The desire to have what does not belong to us destroys. Every time. The story of the two hermits illuminates one of the central ways in which relationships break down: One person's envy of the other opens a door through which death walks in. We desire *their* money, *their* possessions, *their* power; we covet *their* relationships, *their* connections, *their* opportunities; we look with pain in our hearts upon all the good that has come to *them* and wonder what is wrong with *us*. No relationship can long survive the poisonous presence of envy.

The intertestamental book the *Wisdom of Solomon* reminds us that the tragic episode between Cain and Abel wasn't the first time that envy reared its ugly head in God's good world:

> *God created us for incorruption,*
> *and made us in the image of his own eternity,*
> but through the devil's envy death entered the world,
> and those who belong to his company experience it.
> WISDOM 2:23-24, NRSV[4]

According to the *Wisdom of Solomon*, the devil's envy of God led to his cruel scheme to undermine humanity's relationship with

God. And what is more, *the very tool he used to undermine that relationship was envy*. Think about the serpent's words to Eve in the Garden: "You will not die; for God knows that when you eat of it your eyes will be opened, *and you will be like God, knowing good and evil* (Genesis 3:4-5, emphasis mine). The tragedy, of course, is not only that Adam and Eve were *already* "like God"—created in the image and likeness of God—but also that God, who is both good and generous, would have given them everything they needed to know about good and evil exactly when and where it was appropriate. The daily bread of practical knowledge would have been theirs, had they only trusted. Generous God gladly shares, as Jesus reminds us: "All I have is yours, and all you have is mine" (John 17:10).

But instead, like Cain, they murdered God in their hearts. And that is what envy always does. It sunders; it divides; it murders. As the apostle James said,

> What causes fights and quarrels among you? Don't they come from your desires that battle within you? You desire but do not have, so you kill. You covet but you cannot get what you want, so you quarrel and fight. You do not have because you do not ask God. When you ask, you do not receive, because you ask with wrong motives, that you may spend what you get on your pleasures.
>
> JAMES 4:1-3

James would know. He was the half-brother of Jesus and watched as his brother, because of the envy of the Jewish leaders (Mark 15:10; Matthew 27:18), was handed over to Pontius Pilate to suffer and to die. They wanted his influence with the people, his power; they feared the loss of theirs; and from the root of envy came the fruit of murder—Cain's sin writ large. Is there a clearer example of how the desire for what is not ours—and the fear that we will be left without—sunders us from one another and from the life of God than the jealous murder of the man who is God, Jesus the Lord?

And once again, their sin repeats the tragedy of the Garden—for the lordship of Jesus takes away nothing we need but only adds and adds and adds more to who and what we are, until we finally share, each of us and all together, in the life of God and all things in God. By faith, we are made joint heirs of all things with Christ (Romans 8:17). And because of this, Paul can say to the Corinthian Christians, whose existence as a community was constantly threatened by envious factions, "All things are yours, whether Paul or Apollos or Cephas or the world or life or death or the present or the future—all are yours, and you are of Christ, and Christ is of God" (1 Corinthians 3:21-23). When we realize that everything already belongs to *all of us*, envy is fundamentally unnecessary.

BREAKING ENVY

What, then, is to be done about this desire for what is not ours, which severs us from God and one another, cutting us off from the gracious flow of divine life?

The medieval Italian poet Dante Alighieri wrestled with this question in his famous work, *The Divine Comedy*, in which he figuratively maps the soul's sojourn out of the death of sin and into the life of God, telling a story of his journey through hell and purgatory and finally to paradise. In purgatory, he meets those who in this life had been conquered by the sin of envy: souls who "rejoiced far more at others' hurts / than at [their] own good fortune."[5] For these souls, the punishment (which also will be their healing) is to have their eyes sewn shut with wires so that they can no longer look upon the lives of others with envy, nor compare those lives with theirs.

The fathers and mothers of the desert would heartily agree that one of the most spiritually healthy things we can do is to simply stop paying attention to what others have (and what we do or don't have in comparison) since the result can really only be one of two things: Either we are filled with pride that we have more than others, or we are filled with anger and sadness that we have less than others. Both are spiritually disastrous. One fills us with a false confidence in ourselves; the other cuts gratitude at the root—and both sever us from the life of God. So part of the solution here is that we need to start to learn to say once again with the psalmist,

> Lord, you alone are my portion and my cup;
>   you make my lot secure.
> The boundary lines have fallen for me in pleasant places;
>   surely I have a delightful inheritance.
> PSALM 16:5-6

And then, saying this, we must "sew our eyes shut" to what others have, remembering that happiness isn't having everything we want but, rather, *wanting* everything that we *have*—cultivating a spirit of contentment within the "boundary lines" the Lord has assigned to us. In this way, Saint Augustine's words will prove true of us: "Happy is he who has all he desires, and desires nothing amiss"[6]—which works *only on the presumption that our desires have been sanctified*. When we are content with God, inside the lives he has given us, we are happy. When we are not, we are miserable.

More of us, quite honestly, need to practice this. We would

do well to remember, with the writer of Ecclesiastes, that so much of our "toil and all achievement spring from one person's envy of another" (Ecclesiastes 4:4). We work ourselves to the bone not because we *need* to but because we're trying to keep up with the lifestyles of the rich and famous—or, closer to home, our friends, who seem to always be making *just a little bit more* money than we are. How foolish. And unnecessary. What if, instead, we slowed down, took some deep breaths, gave thanks to God for the good things he has given us, for the people he has surrounded us with, and then entered enjoyment of them? That, friend, is the daily invitation of the Lord. And it goes a long way toward cutting the root of envy.

But given our fallen condition, attitude adjustments will likely prove to be not quite enough. And so the Desert Fathers and Mothers counsel us to actively break the lordship of possessiveness over our lives. "The desire for possessions," said Abba Isidore of Pelusia, "is dangerous and terrible, knowing no satiety; it drives the soul which it controls to the heights of evil. Therefore let us drive it away vigorously from the beginning. For once it has become master it cannot be overcome."[7]

And how do we do that? Jesus said that if our hand or foot caused us to sin, we should chop it off and throw it away (Matthew 18:8). Something like that is at work in the desert counsel to divest ourselves—as much as we are able—of unnecessary possessions. If the desire for things—money and possessions, but even status, power, and certain relationships—is a source of sin, then the obvious thing to do is simply to "chop it off"; that is, to renounce it. To lay it down, to let it go, to walk the other direction, to choose a new path.

And when we step out of the endless cycle of envy and greed and accumulation of unnecessary possessions—we experience the joy and freedom of the Kingdom! As Jesus said to the rich young ruler, "You will have treasure in heaven." You might recall here the story of Abba Agathon and his disciples from earlier on in this book. Agathon's disciples were dismayed at his cavalier abandonment of a cell that he had spent a great deal of time working on, protesting to him that he'd be thought unstable. Agathon's response? "If some are scandalized, others, on the contrary, will be much edified and will say, 'How blessed are they who go away for God's sake, having no other care.'"

We need a new training in righteousness, friend. Beyond simply being *grateful* for what we have, many of us would do well to relearn the art of *abandoning* what we have for the sake of the Kingdom— the art of *letting go* of whatever has us bound with obsession and worry and compulsion so that we can *lay hold* of God.

Perhaps it is time to exit the rat race, once and for all. To say no to the promotion that promises more money but will steal time from your family or diminish your peace of mind. To sell the house that impresses your friends but is twice as large as you need (and difficult to keep up with financially). To stop yielding to the compulsive need to have new vehicles and start purchasing used, so that you have more resources to share with others. And to do all of this and more as acts of worship. Maybe it's time for us to begin to learn to live simply, and humbly, and reverently again, breaking the stranglehold of envy on our lives.

RADICAL GENEROSITY

And still, there is more.

When I first began to wrestle with the sayings and stories of the desert, one of the things I quickly noticed was how often some version of a story like this came up:

The same old man [Abba Euprepius] helped some thieves when they were stealing. When they had taken away what was inside his cell, Abba Euprepius saw that they had left his stick and he was sorry. So he took it and ran after them to give it to them. But the thieves did not want to take it, fearing that something would happen to them if they did. So he asked someone he met who was going the same way to give the stick to them.[8]

Now who does a thing like that—assisting thieves as they plunder your goods? "Madness!" we want to cry. And indeed Euprepius's total madness is manifest in his determination to make sure that the thieves would take *all* that had belonged to him—which he seems to do with a kind of wink and a smile. "Oh, you think you're going to outsmart me in this?"—and then ensures that even his walking stick goes with them. *Euprepius must be crazy*, we think. Or is he?

A similar story is told of Abba Macarius:

The same Abba Macarius while he was in Egypt discovered a man who owned a beast of burden engaged in plundering Macarius' goods. So he came up to the thief as if he was a stranger and he helped him to load the animal. He saw him off in great peace of soul, saying, "We have brought nothing into this world, and we cannot take anything out of the world." (1 Tim 6.7) "The Lord gave and the Lord has taken away; blessed be the name of the Lord." (Job 1.21).[9]

Once again, Macarius, like Euprepius, willingly and even gratefully enters the plundering, using it as a doorway to move beyond the surface of life to its depths. To the extent that Macarius blesses the thief with all he is and has, he enjoys "great peace of soul," for he is experiencing something of the depths of God that cannot be experienced in any other way.

This kind of radicality marks the Desert Fathers and Mothers:

> A brother saw Abba Nisterius wearing two tunics and he questioned him, saying, "If a poor man came to ask you for a tunic, which would you give him?" He replied, "The better one." "And if someone else asked you for one, what would you give him?" The old man said, "Half of the other one." The brother said, "And if someone else asked for one, what would you give him?" He said, "I should cut the rest, give him half, and gird myself with whatever was left." So the brother said, "And if someone came and asked you for that, what would you do?" The old man said, "I would give him the rest and go and sit down somewhere, until God sent me something to cover myself with."[10]

What kind of spiritual vision makes possible a generosity this outrageous—a generosity that will joyfully give and give and give, until there is nothing left? What *motivated* the Desert Fathers and Mothers to abandon possessions the way they did? Once we grasp this, we'll arrive at the throbbing heart of the Kingdom, the source from which life-giving streams flow, even in the wilderness.

THE CEASELESS FLOW

In the last few years, I've found great solace in taking regular, solitary walks through the neighborhood. I indulge this practice daily, sometimes multiple times a day. In the morning always, usually in the evening, and sometimes in the middle of the day, if I can steal away.

My favorite little walk is on a dirt path behind my house that slices between the boundary of my neighborhood and a cow pasture owned by a local cattle rancher. A stream inside the rancher's property runs parallel to the boundary, and when I make the turn off the sidewalk onto the path and begin to hear the quiet song of the water running over the rocks, something in me settles. I love that moment.

Since I make the walk daily, I've become attuned to the way the seasons manifest their peculiar glory. As I write this, it is early June, and the landscape that surrounds the path is as green as it will be all year. *Verdant* is a bit of a high-browed word for it, but I like it. Everything is *verdant*. The grass is a rich green, the trees have put forth confident leaves, and there are flowers everywhere.

Two weekends ago, the lilacs and all their blossomy friends exploded, perfuming the air with their gladness. As I walked the path and the surrounding neighborhood, I drank it in. Every time I passed a blossomed tree or a shrub, I would stick my face in it and close my eyes and draw in deep draughts of that miraculous, healing aroma—nature lavishing her gifts with no strings attached, ravishing as she puts forth abundant life.

But even now, small signs of what is to come are around me. Those blossoms already have fallen. And though I know it is several months off, before long the leaves will change and fall. The verdant grass will slowly turn various shades of brown. The nights will lengthen, the days will shorten, the air will become colder, and the "giving" of this year will be complete. All the living things will enter the deep darkness of winter to gather up new strength to put forth the gift again next year, made possible by the one who, as Rilke said, "with infinite tenderness holds this falling in his hands."[11]

All of this is a roundabout way of saying: I am learning something on these walks. It is pushing its way down to the roots of my being, and it is changing me.

I am learning that whatever it is we mean by "life," we must mean this ceaseless flow of total receiving and total giving. I am learning that what is true of the stream is true of the grass and the trees and the blossoms, and the rest of God's good world—my life included, and yours. That as the stream *just is* the total passing through of the water, the receiving *and* the giving, the coming *and* the going, so it is for the entire cosmos, and for us—we *receive* life from Life and yield that life to Life, and so we live. Thus Mary Oliver's insistence that life is "praising"; that it is "giving until the giving feels like receiving."[12]

And I am also learning this—that whatever it is we mean by "death" must surely be the cessation of this process in us, whether by choice, accident, or necessity. *We live—only and exactly—to the extent that we receive and then give.* It is that simple. And this is what folks like Euprepius and Macarius and Nisterius, along with the rest of the Desert Fathers and Mothers, are trying to teach us. Our lives are not our own. No life is. Every life finds its complete consummation in the total gift of itself. In the receiving and the giving.

At the heart of the Christian message is the claim that "God so loved the world that he gave his one and only Son, that whoever believes in him would not perish but have eternal life" (John 3:16). For John, the story of Jesus is the story of the infinite generosity of God, which culminates in Jesus' total gift of himself on the cross, and which also makes us alive—the Life of God poured out for the life of the world.

"Life itself," writes Father John O'Donohue, "is the primal sacrament, namely, *the* visible sign of invisible grace. The structures of our experience are the windows into the divine."[13] Or as the psalmist put it more simply, "The heavens declare the glory of God" (Psalm 19:1). What I am learning from the created order about the nature of life is true about *life* because it was and is true about *Life* first.

For God in himself is the giving that knows no end. The Father from all eternity pours forth his being, and that pouring forth is the Son. And the Son from all eternity receives being from the Father and pours it back upon him, creating a ceaseless flow of giving and receiving we call the Holy Spirit—the personal dynamic life of the tripersonal God, proceeding from the Father and the Son, with the Father and Son worshiped and glorified.

And from the depths of the triune life all things were made, not only as a mirror and analogy of that one divine life but as participants in it, living and moving and having their being in the One whose infinite life knows no end (Acts 17:28). Thomas Traherne wrote that God is "the primitive eternal spring / the endless ocean of each glorious thing" from which all things "run like rivers from, into the main" and "all it doth receive returns again."[14] The destiny of all things, says Traherne, is to yield their being to Being, to yield their lives completely and utterly to God—the one unbroken, triune life, the ceaseless divine giving and receiving—and therefore to truly live.

It is *that* divine life—extravagantly and absolutely generous—that Jesus makes manifest in his sojourn from Bethlehem to Golgotha: "The Son of Man did not come to be served, but to serve, *and to give his life as a ransom for many*" (Matthew 20:28, emphasis mine). And the staggering claim of the New Testament is that to be God's people is not just to be *saved by* that extravagant and absolute generosity but to be *saved for* it:

> But whatever were gains to me I now consider loss for the sake of Christ. What is more, I consider everything a loss because of the surpassing worth of knowing Christ Jesus my Lord, for whose sake I have lost all things. I consider them garbage, that I may gain Christ and be found in him, not having a righteousness of my own that comes from the law, but that which is through faith in Christ— the righteousness that comes from God on the basis of faith. I want to know Christ—yes, to know the power of his resurrection and participation in his sufferings, becoming like him in his death, and so, somehow, attaining to the resurrection from the dead.
>
> PHILIPPIANS 3:7-11

For the apostle Paul, what this *looked like* was the total gift of himself to the people God had called him to; to the churches he loved and served; and to the Gentiles, for whom the doors of the Kingdom had been thrown wide open. As Christ Jesus gave his life for the life of the world and was gathered up by the Father into Resurrection life, so Paul believed that conformity to Christ Jesus meant giving his own life for the life of the world and being gathered up by the Father into the resurrection life of God—into that life that simply *is* Life, the endless giving and receiving that is the eternally replete, infinitely flowered life of the Triune God.

This is what is at stake in the desert's witness to generosity and why I think it represents the full flowering of their spiritual vision—for the life *rooted* in the God made known in Jesus will find itself *fruited* in the way that God's own life is infinitely fruited: in the love and life that is manifest in the complete gift of itself for the life of others. We show ourselves to be the body of the Christ who is the body of God in the world—or, as Karl Barth put it, "the earthly body of the heavenly Lord"[15]—when we live as he lived: poured out for the life of the world, our fruit given as food and our leaves for the healing of the nations (Revelation 22:2).

A WORD FOR OUR TIME

And this, I think, is also a prophetic call for our day. We live in a spiritual wasteland because we have forgotten this—if indeed we ever really knew it. We are a wasteland because in a thousand ways we have lost touch with the most fundamental truths of the divine-human life that God has created for us in Jesus Christ, burying the generous, endless, life-giving streams of God under the rubble of noise and hurry and distraction, of fear and anger and selfishness, and the ground is now weary and very dry.

If there is any hope, therefore, for the renewal of our culture, the Desert Fathers and Mothers remind us that it will not come through a church bent on protecting itself from the world. Nor will it come from a moralizing church spouting judgment at the world—and least of all from a church trying to "take back" the culture from the world. All of these being so much rubble and chief contributors to the desolation of our age.

No, renewal won't come that way. The Desert Fathers and Mothers remind us that it will come in one way and one way alone: namely, from a church that is willing to be pierced and plundered—as Jesus' body was pierced and plundered. From a church that is willing to hang vulnerably amid the reek of injustice, speaking words of healing and blessing—as Jesus hung vulnerably amid the reek, speaking blessing. From a church that would rather die for its enemies than see its enemies put to death—as Jesus died in the place of his enemies to make them friends.

From a church, in short, that lives and loves like Jesus lives and loves—even unto death.

So be it.

Acknowledgments

A book is always a community effort, and as such, I have many people to thank.

To the wonderful team at NavPress—Dave, Caitlyn, and Elizabeth: You guys are a dream to work with, an answer to prayer. Thanks for helping to bring this idea to fruition.

To my agent, Alex Field, and the entire team at The Bindery: I can't tell you how much I appreciate you. Thanks for taking a chance on a no-name aspiring author back in 2017. I'm indebted.

To whomever it was who first recommended I read Benedicta Ward's collection of sayings from the desert: Thank you. Not every book changes your life, but that one changed mine. (If and when you identify yourself, lunch is on me. Forever.)

To my colleagues and brothers at New Life—Brady, Glenn, Daniel, Brian, Brad, Jon, Jason, and Pete: Your faithfulness to the way of Jesus and your deep care for God's people have made me a better man and pastor in every way. I love each of you.

To the staff and congregation of New Life East: You might be the biggest (and happiest) surprise of my life to this point. The

Spirit has used your love and encouragement to work a resurrection for me. I can't believe I get to share life with you. Let's keep going.

To the good people of Believer's Church in Marshfield, Wisconsin (circa 1981–1999), to whom this book is dedicated: The holiness and devotion you modeled left a deep mark on me. As I've said before (and say again here): Your witness has been with me every day of the last fifteen years of my ministry. I pray that ministry (and this book!) honors you.

To my parents, Bill and Nancy, and my siblings—John, Anna, and Robert: I couldn't be blessed with a better group of people to call family. I love each of you.

And to Mandi and our four kids—Ethan, Gabe, Bella, and Liam: Being a husband and "dad" is the absolute greatest privilege of my life, my constant joy. "The boundary lines have fallen for me in pleasant places; surely I have a delightful inheritance" (Psalm 16:6). That's you. Thanks for loving (and putting up with!) me.

Notes

FOREWORD

1. St. Maximos the Confessor, *On Difficulties in Sacred Scripture: The Responses to Thalassios*, trans. Fr. Maximos Constas (Washington, DC: Catholic University of America Press, 2018), 21.4.
2. Maximos, *On Difficulties*, 21.6.

INTRODUCTION: STANDING AT THE CROSSROADS

1. Alexander Schmemann, *For the Life of the World: Sacraments and Orthodoxy* (Crestwood, New York: St. Vladimir's, 1973), 14.
2. Saint Augustine, *Confessions*, trans. Henry Chadwick (Oxford: Oxford University Press, 2008), 3.
3. Rainer Maria Rilke, in *The Poetry of Rilke*, trans. and ed. Edward Snow (New York: Farrar, Straus, and Giroux, 2009), 9.
4. Juvenal, Satire X.
5. As quoted by Alan Kreider, *The Patient Ferment of the Early Church: The Improbable Rise of Christianity in the Roman Empire* (Grand Rapids, MI: Baker Academic, 2016), 58.
6. As quoted in Kreider, *Patient Ferment*, 67.
7. I owe this insight to David Bentley Hart, *Atheist Delusions: The Christian Revolution and Its Fashionable Enemies* (New Haven, CT: Yale University Press, 2009), 241.
8. Archbishop Anthony of Sourzah, in the preface to Benedicta Ward, trans., *The Sayings of the Desert Fathers: The Alphabetical Collection* (Kalamazoo, MI: Cistercian, 1984), xv–xvi.
9. Hart, *Atheist Delusions*, 240.

10. As quoted in Ward, *Sayings*, 133.
11. Ward, *Sayings*, 230.
12. Ward, *Sayings*, 189.
13. Ward, *Sayings*, 83.
14. Felix Timmermans, *The Perfect Joy of Saint Francis: A Novel*, trans. L. A. Aspelagh (San Francisco: Ignatius Press, 1998), 84.
15. Henri Nouwen, *The Way of the Heart* (New York: Ballantine Books, 2003).
16. Andrew Arndt, *All Flame: Entering into the Life of the Father, Son, and Holy Spirit* (Colorado Springs: NavPress, 2020).
17. Ward, *Sayings*, 9.
18. Ward, *Sayings*, 85–86.
19. Ward, *Sayings*, 44.
20. Thomas Merton, *Thoughts in Solitude* (New York: Noonday, 1995), 20.
21. Ward, *Sayings*, 6.
22. Wendell Berry, *The Selected Poems of Wendell Berry*, "The Mad Farmer Manifesto: The First Amendment" (Berkeley, CA: Counterpoint, 1998), 89.

CHAPTER 1: FOR THE LOVE OF GOD

1. John Cassian, *Conferences* (Mahwah, NJ: Paulist Press, 1985), 37.
2. Cassian, *Conferences*, 39.
3. Cassian, *Conferences*, 41.
4. Cassian, *Conferences*, 42, 44–45.
5. As told in Benedicta Ward, trans., *The Sayings of the Desert Fathers: The Alphabetical Collection* (Kalamazoo, MI: Cistercian, 1984), 31.
6. Ward, *Sayings*, 3–4.
7. Ward, *Sayings*, 3.
8. Rowan Williams, *Where God Happens: Discovering Christ in One Another* (Boston: New Seeds, 2005), 24. Emphasis mine.
9. Williams, *Where God Happens*, 33.
10. Ward, *Sayings*, 27.
11. Ward, *Sayings*, 23.
12. Ward, *Sayings*, 142–143.
13. Greg Lukianoff and Jonathan Haidt, *The Coddling of the American Mind: How Good Intentions and Bad Ideas Are Setting Up a Generation for Failure* (New York: Penguin Books, 2018).
14. Ward, *Sayings*, 153.
15. Martin Luther King Jr., *Strength to Love* (Philadelphia: Fortress, 1981), 56.
16. Cassian, *Conferences*, 58. Emphasis mine.

CHAPTER 2: THE GREAT RENUNCIATION

1. As told in Benedicta Ward, trans., *The Sayings of the Desert Fathers: The Alphabetical Collection* (Kalamazoo, MI: Cistercian, 1984), 21.
2. Ward, *Sayings*, 42.
3. Ward, *Sayings*, 218.
4. John Cassian, *Conferences* (Mahwah, NJ: Paulist Press, 1985), 83.
5. Cassian, *Conferences*, 83.
6. Cassian, *Conferences*, 83.
7. Cassian, *Conferences*, 85.
8. I spoke at length about this in my book *All Flame*.
9. Cassian, *Conferences*, 85.
10. Julian of Norwich, *Showings*, trans. Edmund Colledge and James Walsh (Mahwah, NJ: Paulist, 1978), 167–170.
11. Thomas Merton, *The Seven Storey Mountain: An Autobiography of Faith* (New York: Harcourt, 1999), 246.
12. Merton, *Seven Storey Mountain*, 242.
13. Cassian, *Conferences*, 88.
14. Merton, *Seven Storey Mountain*, 351.
15. Merton, *Seven Storey Mountain*, 462.
16. Thomas Merton, *New Seeds of Contemplation* (New York: New Directions, 2007), 268.
17. Ronald Rolheiser, *Sacred Fire: A Vision for a Deeper Human and Christian Maturity* (New York: Image, 2014), 68–72.
18. Ward, *Sayings*, 194.

CHAPTER 3: ESSENTIAL HABITS FOR THE WITH-GOD LIFE

1. Julian of Norwich, *Showings*, trans. Edmund Colledge and James Walsh (Mahwah, NJ: Paulist, 1978), 212.
2. As told in Benedicta Ward, trans., *The Sayings of the Desert Fathers: The Alphabetical Collection* (Kalamazoo, MI: Cistercian, 1984), 9.
3. Ward, *Sayings*, 92.
4. Ward, *Sayings*, 9.
5. Ward, *Sayings*, 139.
6. As quoted in Rowan Williams, *Where God Happens: Discovering Christ in One Another* (Boston: New Seeds, 2005), 121.
7. Ward, *Sayings*, 3.
8. "Preaching Moment 012: Walter Brueggemann," WorkingPreacher, September 23, 2008, https://www.youtube.com/watch?v=J5nPlPMDDQ0.
9. Thanks to my friend Kenneth Tanner for putting it this way.

10. Henri Nouwen, *The Way of the Heart* (New York: Ballantine Books, 2003), 11–12.
11. Nouwen, *Way of the Heart*, 15–16.
12. Ward, *Sayings*, 21–22.
13. Ward, *Sayings*, 76. Emphasis mine.
14. Williams, *Where God Happens*, 70.
15. For an outrageously good exploration of this theme, see Chris Green's magnificent work *Sanctifying Interpretation: Vocation, Holiness, and Scripture,* 2nd ed. (Cleveland, TN: CPT Press, 2020), especially part one.
16. Dietrich Bonhoeffer, *Life Together* (New York: Harper, 1954), 21.
17. Bonhoeffer, *Life Together*, 76.
18. Thomas à Kempis, *The Imitation of Christ* (New York: Vintage Books, 1998), 27.
19. Bonhoeffer, *Life Together*, 76.
20. Bonhoeffer, *Life Together*, 77.
21. Bonhoeffer, *Life Together*, 77–78.
22. Mother Teresa, *Where There Is Love, There Is God: A Path to Closer Union with God and Greater Love for Others*, ed. Brian Kolodiejchuk (New York: Image, 2010), 16.
23. As quoted by Robert Louis Wilken, *The Spirit of Early Christian Thought: Seeking the Face of God* (New Haven, CT: Yale University Press, 2003), 50.

CHAPTER 4: CALLED TO COMMUNITY

1. Not their real names.
2. *The Hebrew and Aramaic Lexicon of the Old Testament*, Accordance ed., version 12.3.7 (desktop program, 2020), s.v. "bārak."
3. Walter Brueggemann, "Blessing" in *Reverberations of Faith: A Theological Handbook of Old Testament Themes* (Louisville, KY: John Knox Press, 2002), 18–19.
4. Owen Chadwick, from the introduction to John Cassian, *Conferences* (Mahwah, NJ: Paulist Press, 1985), 5.
5. Cassian, *Conferences*, 54.
6. Cassian, *Conferences*, 61.
7. Cassian, *Conferences*, 64.
8. Cassian, *Conferences*, 65.
9. Cassian, *Conferences*, 64.
10. Cassian, *Conferences*, 67. Emphasis mine.
11. Cassian, *Conferences*, 71–74.
12. As told in Benedicta Ward, trans., *The Sayings of the Desert Fathers: The Alphabetical Collection* (Kalamazoo, MI: Cistercian, 1984), 85–86.

CHAPTER 5: SAVED INTO COMMUNITY

1. Rowan Williams, *Where God Happens: Discovering Christ in One Another* (Boston: New Seeds, 2005), 130.
2. As told in Benedicta Ward, trans., *The Desert Fathers: Sayings of the Early Christian Monks* (New York: Penguin Books, 2003), 134–135.
3. Ward, *Desert Fathers*, 137.
4. Catherine of Siena, *The Dialogue* (Mahwah, NJ: Paulist, 1980), 62.
5. Robert W. Jenson, *Systematic Theology Volume 2: The Works of God* (New York: Oxford University Press, 1999), 212–213.
6. Augnet.org, "2343 totus christus," accessed December 2, 2021, http://www.augnet.org/en/works-of-augustine/his-ideas/theology /2343-totus-christus/.
7. Mother Teresa, *A Simple Path*, comp. Lucinda Vardey (New York: Ballantine Books, 1995), 79.
8. Thomas Merton, *New Seeds of Contemplation* (New York: New Directions, 2007), 65.
9. My dear friend Daniel Grothe has written an exceptional book exploring this theme called *The Power of Place: Choosing Stability in a Rootless Age* (Nashville: Thomas Nelson, 2021).
10. As told in Benedicta Ward, trans., *The Sayings of the Desert Fathers: The Alphabetical Collection* (Kalamazoo, MI: Cistercian, 1984), 231.
11. Ward, *Sayings*, 2.
12. Bessel van der Kolk, *The Body Keeps the Score: Brain, Mind, and Body in the Healing of Trauma* (New York: Penguin Viking, 2014), 38.
13. "A brother came to Abba Theodore and began to converse with him about things which he had never yet put into practice. So the old man said to him, 'You have not yet found a ship nor put your cargo aboard it and before you have sailed, you have already arrived at the city. Do the work first; then you will have the speed you are making now'" (Ward, *Sayings*, 75).
14. John O'Donohue, *Anam Ċara: A Book of Celtic Wisdom* (New York: HarperCollins, 1998).
15. Ward, *Sayings*, 191.

CHAPTER 6: RESTORED THROUGH COMMUNITY

1. As told in Benedicta Ward, trans., *The Sayings of the Desert Fathers: The Alphabetical Collection* (Kalamazoo, MI: Cistercian, 1984), 179–180.
2. See also Isaiah 42:1-4.
3. Ward, *Sayings*, 42.
4. Ward, *Sayings*, 6.

5. Ward, *Sayings*, 28–29.

6. Ward, *Sayings*, 96.

7. Ward, *Sayings*, 24.

8. Ward, *Sayings*, 24.

9. My friend Glenn Packiam has written a brilliant book on this theme called *Blessed, Broken, Given: How Your Story Becomes Sacred in the Hands of Jesus* (Colorado Springs: Multnomah, 2019).

10. This appears to be a mashup of things Saint Augustine said and believed. Part of it is from his sermon 272. See also footnote 2 here: https://revivingcreation.org/behold-what-you-are-become -what-you-receive/.

11. Dietrich Bonhoeffer, *Sanctorum Communio: A Theological Study of the Sociology of the Church* (Minneapolis: Fortress Press, 2009), 140, 138.

12. Robert W. Jenson, *Systematic Theology, Volume 2: The Works of God* (New York: Oxford University Press, 1999), 222.

13. Dietrich Bonhoeffer, *Life Together* (New York: Harper, 1954), 21.

14. Ward, *Sayings*, 138–139.

15. Dallas Willard, *The Divine Conspiracy* (San Francisco: Harper, 1998), 223.

16. Willard, *Divine Conspiracy*, 217–218.

17. Bonhoeffer, *Life Together*, 23.

18. Bonhoeffer, *Life Together*, 26.

19. Ward, *Sayings*, 93.

20. Ward, *Sayings*, 204.

21. Ward, *Sayings*, 108.

CHAPTER 7: SAVING SPEECH

1. As told in Benedicta Ward, trans., *The Sayings of the Desert Fathers: The Alphabetical Collection* (Kalamazoo, MI: Cistercian, 1984), 9.

2. Rowan Williams, *Where God Happens: Discovering Christ in One Another* (Boston: New Seeds, 2005), 41.

3. Ward, *Sayings*, 20.

4. Richard J. Foster, *Celebration of Discipline: The Path to Spiritual Growth* (New York: HarperSanFrancisco, 1998), 101.

5. Ward, *Sayings*, 238.

6. Henri Nouwen, *The Way of the Heart* (New York: Ballantine Books, 2003), 38–39.

7. Ward, *Sayings*, 131.

8. Ward, *Sayings*, 141.

9. Ward, *Sayings*, 141.

10. Dallas Willard, *The Divine Conspiracy* (San Francisco: Harper, 1998), 224.
11. From the Book of Common Prayer. The Holy Eucharist—A Penitential Order: Rite Two.
12. Dr. Cornel West, interview by Anderson Cooper, CNN, June 10, 2020, https://www.youtube.com/watch?v=tTUNIqHRsH8&fbclid=IwAR1xHyK f70brdvT88iz6UE1ff0l2HssjFCxUanomcpgxs0S1Cj9ZR3hute4&app =desktop.
13. James H. Cone, *The Cross and the Lynching Tree* (Maryknoll, New York: Orbis Books, 2017), 28.
14. Ward, *Sayings*, 198.
15. Ward, *Sayings*, 122.
16. Ward, *Sayings*, 236.
17. Ward, *Sayings*, 171. Emphasis mine.
18. Foster, *Celebration of Discipline*, 98.
19. Ward, *Sayings*, 175.
20. Ward, *Sayings*, 98.
21. Williams, *Where God Happens*, 42.
22. Ward, *Sayings*, 98.

CHAPTER 8: SANCTIFYING WORK

1. As told in Benedicta Ward, trans., *The Sayings of the Desert Fathers: The Alphabetical Collection* (Kalamazoo, MI: Cistercian, 1984), 2.
2. Ward, *Sayings*, 188.
3. Ward, *Sayings*, 249.
4. "John Cassian. *Institutes* Book X. Of the Spirit of Accidie," accessed November 2, 2021, http://medieval.ucdavis.edu/120A/Cassian.html.
5. Ward, *Sayings*, 86.
6. Ward, *Sayings*, 6.
7. Dorothy Sayers, "Why Work?" accessed November 2, 2021, https://www1. villanova.edu/content/dam/villanova/mission/faith /Why%20Work%20by%20Dorothy%20Sayers.pdf, 6–7.
8. Wendell Berry, 2002 poem X in *This Day: Collected and New Sabbath Poems* (Berkeley, CA: Counterpoint, 2013), 235.
9. Wendell Berry, *Jayber Crow* (Berkeley, CA: Counterpoint, 2000), 54.
10. Ward, *Sayings*, 120–121.
11. Pope John Paul II, *Laborem Exercens* (Boston: Pauline, 1981), 23.
12. Ward, *Sayings*, 194.
13. Pope John Paul II, *Laborem*, 58.
14. As quoted by Alan Kreider, *The Patient Ferment of the Early Church: The*

Improbable Rise of Christianity in the Roman Empire (Grand Rapids, MI: Baker Academic, 2016), 100.

CHAPTER 9: DIVINE GENEROSITY

1. As told in Benedicta Ward, trans., *The Sayings of the Desert Fathers: The Alphabetical Collection* (Kalamazoo, MI: Cistercian, 1984), 73.
2. Ward, *Sayings*, 22.
3. Benedicta Ward, trans., *The Desert Fathers: Sayings of the Early Christian Monks* (New York: Penguin Books, 2003), xv.
4. Emphasis mine.
5. Dante Alighieri, *The Divine Comedy*, Purgatorio: Canto XIII, lines 110–111.
6. St. Augustine of Hippo, *De Trinitate*, book 13, chapter 5.
7. Ward, *Sayings*, 99.
8. Ward, *Sayings*, 62.
9. Ward, *Sayings*, 131.
10. Ward, *Sayings*, 154–155.
11. Rainer Maria Rilke, "Autumn," in *The Poetry of Rilke*, trans. and ed. Edward Snow (New York: Farrar, Straus, and Giroux, 2009), 87.
12. Mary Oliver, "To Begin With: The Sweet Grass" from *Devotions* (Penguin, New York: 2017), 77.
13. John O'Donohue, *To Bless the Space Between Us* (New York: Convergent, 2008), xvi.
14. Thomas Traherne, "The Circulation."
15. Karl Barth, *Church Dogmatics I.2: The Doctrine of the Word of God* (Edinburgh: T&T Clark, 1956), 744.